Tantsi

33 1/3 Global

33 1/3 Global, a series related to but independent from **33 1/3**, takes the format of the original series of short, music-based books and brings the focus to music throughout the world. With initial volumes focusing on Japanese and Brazilian music, the series will also include volumes on the popular music of Australia/Oceania, Europe, Africa, the Middle East, and more.

33 1/3 Japan

Series Editor: Noriko Manabe

Spanning a range of artists and genres—from the 1970s rock of Happy End to technopop band Yellow Magic Orchestra, the Shibuya-kei of Cornelius, classic anime series *Cowboy Bebop,* J-Pop/EDM hybrid Perfume, and vocaloid star Hatsune Miku—33 1/3 Japan is a series devoted to in-depth examination of Japanese popular music of the twentieth and twenty-first centuries.

Published Titles:

Supercell's *Supercell* by Keisuke Yamada

AKB48 by Patrick W. Galbraith and Jason G. Karlin

Yoko Kanno's *Cowboy Bebop Soundtrack* by Rose Bridges

Perfume's *Game* by Patrick St. Michel

Cornelius's *Fantasma* by Martin Roberts

Joe Hisaishi's *My Neighbor Totoro: Soundtrack* by Kunio Hara

Shonen Knife's *Happy Hour* by Brooke McCorkle

Nenes' *Koza Dabasa* by Henry Johnson

Yuming's *The 14th Moon* by Lasse Lehtonen

Forthcoming Titles:

Yellow Magic Orchestra's *Yellow Magic Orchestra* by Toshiyuki Ohwada

Kohaku utagassen: The Red and White Song Contest by Shelley Brunt

33 1/3 Brazil

Series Editor: Jason Stanyek

Covering the genres of samba, tropicália, rock, hip hop, forró, bossa nova, heavy metal, and funk, among others, 33 1/3 Brazil is a series devoted to in-depth examination of the most important Brazilian albums of the twentieth and twenty-first centuries.

Published Titles:

Caetano Veloso's *A Foreign Sound* by Barbara Browning

Tim Maia's *Tim Maia Racional Vols. 1 &2* by Allen Thayer

João Gilberto and Stan Getz's *Getz/Gilberto* by Brian McCann

Gilberto Gil's *Refazenda* by Marc A. Hertzman

Dona Ivone Lara's *Sorriso Negro* by Mila Burns

Milton Nascimento and Lô Borges's *The Corner Club* by Jonathon Grasse

Racionais MCs' *Sobrevivendo no Inferno* by Derek Pardue

Naná Vasconcelos's *Saudades* by Daniel B. Sharp

Chico Buarque's First *Chico Buarque* by Charles A. Perrone

Forthcoming Titles:

Jorge Ben Jor's *África Brasil* by Frederick J. Moehn

33 1/3 Europe

Series Editor: Fabian Holt

Spanning a range of artists and genres, 33 1/3 Europe offers engaging accounts of popular and culturally significant albums of Continental Europe and the North Atlantic from the twentieth and twenty-first centuries.

Published Titles:

Darkthrone's *A Blaze in the Northern Sky* by Ross Hagen

Ivo Papazov's *Balkanology* by Carol Silverman

Heiner Müller and Heiner Goebbels's *Wolokolamsker Chaussee* by Philip V. Bohlman

33 1/3 Oceania

Series Editors: Jon Stratton (senior editor) and Jon Dale (specializing in books on albums from Aotearoa/New Zealand)

Spanning a range of artists and genres from Australian Indigenous artists to Maori and Pasifika artists, from Aotearoa/New Zealand noise music to Australian rock, and including music from Papua and other Pacific islands, 33 1/3 Oceania offers exciting accounts of albums that illustrate the wide range of music made in the Oceania region.

The Front Lawn's *Songs from the Front Lawn* by Matthew Bannister
Bic Runga's *Drive* by Henry Johnson

Tantsi

Maria Sonevytsky

Series Editor: Fabian Holt

BLOOMSBURY ACADEMIC
NEW YORK • LONDON • OXFORD • NEW DELHI • SYDNEY

BLOOMSBURY ACADEMIC
Bloomsbury Publishing Inc
1385 Broadway, New York, NY 10018, USA
50 Bedford Square, London, WC1B 3DP, UK
29 Earlsfort Terrace, Dublin 2, Ireland

BLOOMSBURY, BLOOMSBURY ACADEMIC, and the Diana logo are
trademarks of Bloomsbury Publishing Plc

First published in the United States of America 2023

Epigraph used with permission of the Estate of Oleksandr Yevtushenko.

A catalog record for this book is available from the Library of Congress.

ISBN: HB: 978-1-5013-6312-2
       PB: 978-1-5013-6311-5
       ePDF: 978-1-5013-6314-6
       eBook: 978-1-5013-6313-9

Typeset by RefineCatch Limited, Bungay, Suffolk
Printed and bound in Great Britain

Series: 33 1/3 Europe

To find out more about our authors and books visit www.bloomsbury.com
and sign up for our newsletters.

In my memory, the wild rock-and-roll playgrounds of the second half of the 1980s loom large, the busted chairs, broken windows, the adrenaline in your veins instead of blood, the avalanche-like drive of the turbo-punk-rock machine named VV—and Oleg Skrypka, who flew above the abundantly sweat-covered scene like a circus magician, exchanging his bayan for a trumpet, and the trumpet for the guitar. Prominent in my memory are the overfilled halls, the massive rush, the wild dances of home-grown punks in front of the stage and the drunken assembly of the nonconformists (неформали) *of all colors.*

Oleksandr Yevtushenko,
in *Ukraïna IN ROCK* (2011, 69)

Contents

Figures

Acknowledgments

Back in 2019, I imagined this would be my fun and quick post-tenure book. Instead, it became a daunting and protracted project, delayed first by a global pandemic, and then by the full-scale invasion of Ukraine by Russia in February 2022. Two world historical events with consequences much farther reaching than the delay of a little book about a late Soviet Ukrainian punk record; but a useful reminder, I suppose, that—to paraphrase a Ukrainian proverb—no one knows what awaits them in this wild life.

This book was completed in the first six months of the Russian war of aggression on Ukraine, though the bulk of interviews were completed before February 24, 2022. In those frantic months, several of my interviewees reassured me that this project was still valuable, even though it would do nothing to bring an end to the ongoing madness. I listened back to many of my pre-invasion interviews and marveled at the ability of Ukrainians to find humor in what were already dark times; this capacity to laugh despite it all continues to inspire me. Though I did my best to represent their words and memories accurately, any errors or imprecisions are solely my responsibility.

I acknowledge that what this book presents is a partial account. Many of the stories I relate were told to me by individuals who lived through the turbulent *perebudova* years in late Soviet Ukraine, a time when their priority was making music, art, and fun despite the limited and often ludicrous conditions of daily life. To a significant degree, this book relies on the memories of people who were younger than twenty-five in the 1980s; the music described in this book was part of the soundtrack to those heady years of rapid societal change. Their memories (shared with me between 2019 and 2022) had decades to mature, to harden or soften, to grow rosier around the edges, or more austere. My task was to try to carve a path through this thicket of recollection while staying attuned to the memory politics that might be at play. I attempted this, in part, by triangulating with primary sources from that period, most of which exist outside of official archives but thrive on blogs, YouTube channels, and social media groups.

Between the fall of 2019 and the winter of 2022, I interviewed the following people—named in alphabetical order—often following up with additional interviews or for clarification over various messaging platforms: Gennady Gutgarts, Eugene Hütz, Volodya Ivanov, Sashko Pipa, Elena Prigova, Zhenya Rohachevsky, Oleksandr Rudiachenko, Oleg Skrypka, Kyrylo Stetsenko, and Tatyana Yezhova. Without their participation, this book would have been much more of an exercise in speculation; my debt to each of them is immense. I want to especially thank Sashko Pipa and Oleg Skrypka, the two original band members who gave sanction to this project early on and were indispensable sources and supports throughout the process.

The personal archives of Tatyana Yezhova and Oleksandr Rudiachenko were invaluable. Tatyana Yezhova generously shared of her encyclopedic knowledge of the Kyiv punk scene. Her documentary "Дайте Звук, Будь Ласка!" (roughly translated as "Crank the Sound, Please"!) widens the aperture considerably on the Vopli Vidopliassova-focused story of the Kyiv rock scene that I tell here. Oleksandr Rudiachenko delved back into his late-1980s files and allowed me access to materials that I could not locate elsewhere.

Dmytro Gorin, webmaster of the essential online resource at vopli.blogpost.com responded to my inquiries and helped to connect many of the dots in my research. Inna Renchka, Yuri Shevchuk, and Virlana Tkacz consulted on nuances of terminology and translation; Sashko Pipa and Mykola Usatyi helped with the impossible task of translating VV song lyrics into English. I regret that I was not able to speak with Oleksandr Yevtushenko before his passing in 2020, but the vast trove of music journalism that he produced was essential to shaping this project and, as I came to understand, to boosting VV to pre-eminence in the Kyiv rock scene before they blew up across the USSR. His 2011 book, *Україна IN ROCK*, his many articles, and his website (www.rock-oko.com) are well worth exploring.

Numerous scholars gave powerful feedback on this manuscript in its latter stages. I thank the anonymous reviewer; many of their recommendations are reflected here. This book was always going to be in extended dialogue with Alexei Yurchak's watershed *Everything Was Forever, Until It Was No More*, so having him read the first three chapters was an absolute dream, and helped me sharpen some of my boldest claims. Galina Yarmanova gave deep feedback on the conclusion. David Novak's invitation to present this work at UCSB and Olga Plakhotnik's invitation to Greifswald allowed me to test out some of my interpretations on early audiences of fellow scholars in music studies and cutting-edge Ukrainian studies. Tyler Bickford offered honest advice and a compassionate ear. My late colleague Richard Taruskin listened to my earliest ideas for the structure of the book and encouraged me to chase some of the rabbit holes that I worried would be dead ends; his confidence in this work meant a lot to me. Ryan Gourley provided keen and fresh eyes and assisted with the index in the final stages of the process.

Yuriy Gurzhy offered a generous and critical final read of the manuscript.

This book would not exist if it were not for Fabian Holt's invitation to contribute to the 33 1/3 Europe series. I thank him for his enduring support and patience. Amy Martin, Leah Babb-Rosenfeld, and Rachel Moore at Bloomsbury all graciously shepherded the work through to publication.

Andrew Rossiter and his ace team at Org Music, with Dave Gardner of Infrasonic Sound, have made the first official release of *Tantsi* possible; we are all so grateful. (I tell the story of how Sashko Pipa shared the master tape with me, and its subsequent journey to North America, in the conclusion of this book.)

Franz Nicolay's imprint is all over this; I could not have imagined a more ideal partner for our shared life in writing and music. I thank my Ukrainian family, inherited and chosen, for teaching me to respect Ukrainian culture in its diverse manifestations from my earliest youth up to the present. And I will never forget the first time I played the song "Tantsi" for my children Lesia and Artem, who, like me a generation earlier, were unable to withstand the irresistible beat and erupted into uproarious dance.

I dedicate this book to Ukrainians, in their full, complex, resilient, brilliant glory.

Note on Translation and Transliteration

The politics of language usage in Ukraine are notoriously thorny. During the time frame set in this book (1985 to 1989), the Russian language was dominant in Kyiv—the historic Ukrainian capital city where most of the action in this story took place. Because of Soviet language policies, Russian was widely accepted to be the language of prestige and upward mobility, and therefore became the Soviet *lingua franca* throughout the fifteen republics of the USSR in the post-war period. Today, many Russophone Ukrainians feel themselves to be authentically Ukrainian. In the decades since the album at the heart of this book was released, however, there have been significant shifts towards Ukrainian language use among diverse classes of Ukrainians. Many (though not all) of the people interviewed for this project told me that, in the 1980s, they spoke only Russian to their friends and families. Many switched to Ukrainian consciously, and often with considerable effort, after the Orange Revolution of 2004, or the Maidan Revolution of 2013, or after the Russian full-scale invasion of 2022. In many (but not all) cases, therefore, there has been an intensification of language politics punctuated by recurring Ukrainian political crises in the post-Soviet era. Following the full-scale invasion of Ukraine in February 2022, the survival of the Ukrainian language—along with Ukraine itself as a sovereign entity—has turned existential. For these reasons, I prefer to transliterate terms from the Ukrainian rather than the

Russian whenever appropriate. In some cases, when the Russian-language term has become standardized in English (*perestroika*, for example), I offer the Ukrainian term as well (*perebudova*), since my interlocutors often used the Ukrainian term in interviews. In Ukrainian, I follow the transliteration standards set in 2010. For Russian, I follow the ICAO passport standards set in 2013. Wherever possible, I have honored the transliterated naming conventions preferred by my interlocutors.

Timeline: 1985 to 1989

This timeline represents important developments that took place in the time frame of the book you are about to read. In some cases, dates are precise to the day. In other cases—as with the recording of *Tantsi*, the making of the "Tantsi" music video, and its showing on Soviet television—dates are rough and represent my best guess based on the research I have done.

Events in VV's development and the Soviet Ukrainian rock scene	Political and economic developments in USSR and beyond
1985	
	March: Mikhail Gorbachev becomes General Secretary of the Communist Party of the Soviet Union.
	April 23: Central Committee launches programs of *uskorennia* (acceleration) and *perestroika/ perebudova* (restructuring)
	May: Anti-alcohol campaign introduced; *samohon* (home-made spirits) production rises.

Sept 28: First appearance of *Fonohraf* music pages in Kyiv's *Moloda Gvardia* newspaper.

1986

April 26: first independent Kyiv rock festival at Kyiv University organized by *Fonohraf*; there is no live sound equipment available; VV was not included.

April 26: Chernobyl nuclear accident takes place approximately eighty miles north of Kyiv.

Early May: Sashko Pipa and Yuri Zdorenko, who had been playing together since 1981 in the metal band SOS, hold their first rehearsal with Oleg Skrypka in Skrypka's dorm at the Kyiv Polytechnic University on vul. Metalistiv 5.

June: Censorship protocols loosen as the Eighth Congress of the Soviet Writer's Union kicks off cultural *glasnost* (openness).

Oct 29: Debut '86 Festival with live sound, organized by *Fonohraf*, Ukrainian Youth TV, and V. Kurnashov takes place at club "Dnipro" on Kyiv's Left Bank. Reportedly, "a crowd of 1,200 came to a concert hall that was designed for 800."[1]

---

[1]Romana Bahry, "Rock Culture and Rock Music in Ukraine," in *Rocking the State: Rock Music and Politics in Eastern Europe and Russia*, ed. Sabrina P. Ramet (Boulder: Westview Press, 1994), 246.

Events in VV's development and the Soviet Ukrainian rock scene	Political and economic developments in USSR and beyond

Fall: Edem and Kvartyra #50 unite with the Komsomol to open the Kyiv Rock Club, located at the Palace of Culture "Bilshovyk" (38 Prospect Peremohy).

1987
VV release their first unofficial album *Aiaiaiaiaiai* (Аяяяяяяяяяяпплй).

April: "Rock-Dialogue" festival takes place at the House of the Artist, organized by the Central Committee of the Komsomol of Ukraine (ЦК ЛКСМУ) and the Union of Ukrainian Artists. Organizing committee includes V. Ivanov, along with S. Bybyk, and H. Lytnevskyi (VV are not featured).
Oct: VV starts to sing with Ukrainian language lyrics.[2]

Oct: First VV performance takes place during the pause between films at the film festival "Molodist," organized by V. Ivanov

---

[2]Ibid.

Nov: "Parade of Ensembles" takes place at the Kyiv Rock Club at the concert-dance hall "Suchasnyk" on the one-year anniversary of the Rock Club's founding. This was the second public performance by VV, and they won first place for "Band of the Year" and "Song of the Year" with "Yaroslavna's Lament."

Dec: Rock Artil (Rock Guild), the semi-commercial enterprise organized by V. Ivanov, forms as an alternative to Kyiv Rock Club under the umbrella of the association known as "Experiment." VV, along with Kollezhskyi Asessor and Rabbota XO, break off from the Kyiv Rock Club.

1988
Feb: Rock Artil holds their first rock concert in the dance hall of Holosiivsky Park.

March 23: VV and Kollezhskyi Asessor participate in a "Concert-Taryfikatsia" at the publishing house "Youth."

VV's first concert in Poland, organized by V. Ivanov.

April: First edition of the *samizdat* publication *Huchnomovets'* appears.

Events in VV's development and the Soviet Ukrainian rock scene	Political and economic developments in USSR and beyond
April: The first international festival of rock music, "Peace Action," takes place in the Ukrainian SSR, featuring groups from the USSR, Poland, Hungary, and Holland. The lineup included the three bands of Rock Artil: VV, Kollezhskyi Asessor, and Rabbota XO. The festival was organized by the Kyiv City Committee of the Komsomol, and two cooperatives: "Lira" and "Rock Artil."	
May: Rock Artil performance at international "Rock-Forum Vilnius-88."	
	May 26: Law on Cooperatives (N 8998-XI) allows independent worker-owned cooperatives greater entrepreneurial freedoms and gives cooperatives equal rights with state-run enterprises
June: Rok-Artil performs in Moscow at concerts organized by the youth center "Leisure" (Дозвілля).	
VV are featured in the film Soviet Rock made by the French TV station Antenne-2; their performance includes "Buly Den'ki" (There Were Days), recorded at VDNKh in Moscow.	

Summer: "Tantsi" music video recorded at the Ukrainian Television studios (YT-1) on the Left Bank of Kyiv.[3]

Nov: "Miss Rock USSR" festival showcases women rock performers from the Communist world, under the slogan "there are only girls in rock."

1989
January: VV tour to Poland.

Winter: "Tantsi" music video is shown on the "Musical Video Mill" program hosted by Kyrylo Stetsenko on Ukrainian TV 1.

Feb 5: Artemy Troitsky includes VV and Kollezhskyi Asessor in his top ten alternative bands in the USSR.

Feb: *Tantsi* session in the House of Culture of the Institute of Metallurgy.

---

[3]Though I was not able to find an official date for the making and first screening of the "Tantsi" music video, Kyrylo Stetsenko told me that the "Tantsi" video was almost certainly made in the late summer or early fall of 1988, because in the following year there was a different television presenter who took over Stetsenko's role at the "Musical Video Mill" that aired on Ukrainian Television station No. 1, and after May of 1989 Stetsenko became occupied with the organization of the legendary "Chervona Ruta" festival (personal interview, January 4, 2021). Elena Prigova was also fairly confident that the music video had been recorded in the same time frame. None of the original band members nor fans I consulted could provide any precise dates, and formal state archives yielded little information about 1980s VV.

Events in VV's development and the Soviet Ukrainian rock scene	Political and economic developments in USSR and beyond
Mar 8: VV performs in Moscow with the English post-punk band World Domination Enterprises.	
Mar 29: *Fonohraf* release their first cassette release: VV's *Tantsi*.	
April 7, 1989: The "Tantsi" music video is shown on the popular All-Union television program "Vzgliad" ("The View").[4] Later, it is shown on "Programma A."	
April 14: International Rock Bridge (Интер-Рок-Мост) concert features Sonic Youth and VV at the House of the Book (ДК Книга) in Kyiv.	
The *Fonohraf Digest* appears, edited by O. Rudiachenko and O. Yevtushenko.	
Sept: "Blitz-Parade" festival with VV, Kollezhskyi Asessor, Braty Hadiukiny, and GPD.	
Sept 19–24: First Chervona Ruta festival—featuring music sung exclusively in the Ukrainian language—is held in Chernivtsi. VV perform, though their set is, in Skrypka's words, "disastrous."	
	Nov 9: Fall of the Berlin Wall.

[4]Thanks to Tatyana Yezhova for confirming this in the pages of *Huchnomovets*, vol. 4.

1 Introduction: There Will Be Dances

The popular image in the West is that there are two mighty fighting powers in the Soviet Union: the brave righteous perestroika supporters and the evil and corrupt wallowers in stagnation who try to reverse these developments. In fact, the situation is far more complicated. I know of almost nothing in the Soviet Union that is purely black or white. It's actually all shades of grey, mixed up in total chaos, a real ball of confusion, and everyone is entangled, from the bottom right up to the top.

Artemy Troitsky (in *Tusovka*, 4–5)

The day ends,
It surrenders its hopes to the night.
The workers
Are tired of working.
There are lights,
Bright shining lamps.
Come on, people, in the evening to the club.
There will be dances.
There, there, dances.
Da-da-da, dances.
Dances.[1]

---

[1] Unless otherwise noted, song lyrics have been translated from Ukrainian or Russian in collaboration with Sashko Pipa and Mykola Usatyi. The lyrics translated here were sung originally in Ukrainian.

Singer Oleg Skrypka intones the first two lines of the lyrics with gravity, as though we were at a poetry reading, or watching experimental theater—in a sense, we are. The opening frame of the music video, shot in austere black and white, shows two figures on a featureless white plane. Skrypka is blurred deep in the background but is moving towards the camera. Bass player Sashko Pipa stands immobile on the far-left side of the frame. A skinny electric bass slung over Pipa's shoulder is in sharp focus. A snare drum break erupts, and suddenly all four band members of VV leap into the frame, hurling their bodies across the blank background in spastic time to the beat. When the music pauses, Skrypka recites the next two lines as the other band members wander around: "The workers / Are tired of working." Skrypka's pronunciation of the Ukrainian language text is odd but intriguing—some kind of invented dialect? Again, the riff bursts forth, and the four men dance ecstatically. By now, Skrypka, the singer, has arrived at the front of the frame, in full focus, holding the top half of a retro microphone attached to nothing. His face contorts as he declaims the lines about bright shining lamps. The pace of exchange with the drummer, Serhiy Sakhno, picks up and the absurdist game of punk rock freeze tag continues for another round. The frantic rhythmic outbursts between lines of text hint at the punk noise to come when Skrypka, declaiming the last words of the opening stanza, beckons us to the club. "There will be dances (*tantsi*, танці)."

As he utters the word *tantsi*, the song finally jets into a full band arrangement: power chords, sung vocals, the first refrain. Skrypka's voice is reminiscent of Bobby "Boris" Pickett's delivery of the "Monster Mash," with a dash of David Byrne circa "Once in a Lifetime"—to my ears, at least. His voice, singing "tantsi," is doubled at the higher octave by the guitarist, and the electric

Figure 1.1 *A still from the "Tantsi" music video. Screenshot from YouTube.*

guitar, bass, and drums propel the arrangement. The beat and deadpan aesthetics of "Tantsi" share much in common with the German band Trio's 1982 international hit "Da Da Da," as the original band members readily admit. But where "Da Da Da" is restrained, "Tantsi" is feral, manic, and wild-eyed.

During the refrain (as happened in live performances from this time), two men wearing smocks associated with ordinary Soviet workers enter the frame. They hold a large agitprop-style banner with the nonsensical slogan ТАНЦІ (DANCES) spelled out in blocky white letters.[2] The four musicians dance

---

[2]In one of my interviews with Skrypka, he described the aesthetics of the banner as a "very, very restrained hidden protest," because it so strongly invoked the Soviet banners that everyone was "forced to walk with." "The banner was red, with white letters in the style of the newspaper *Pravda*—the font was Soviet-Soviet—but the meaning was kind of nonsensical (безглуздий), so it was very effective" (June 5, 2019).

around, under, and behind the banner, in a state of gleeful abandon. Then, Yuri Zdorenko, dressed in a "proletarian beret" and striped sailor shirt, steps forward to take a guitar solo.[3] The men in worker's coats frame Zdorenko with the banner for his close-up; the others shimmy and mug in the background. The remaining minute-and-a-half of the video alternates between two contrasting scenes: firstly, of the band standing in a lineup, immobile and serious, playing their unplugged instruments; secondly, of the band moving around the banner and—delightfully, ludicrously—*dancing*.

The band Vopli Vidopliassova, known to fans as VV (pronounced "Ve-Ve"), means "the wailings of Vidopliassov."[4] The comically overwrought name was inspired by a character in the 1859 satire *The Village of Stepanchikovo and Its Inhabitants* by Fyodor Dostoyevsky. In the novel, a footman, Gregory Vidopliassov, becomes obsessed with the idea of writing, and refers to his florid writings as "wailings of the soul." The band's original bass player, Sashko Pipa, was reading the work while the group tried out various band names. He told me that he suggested it first as a joke, but it stuck. The name appealed in part because of the character's combination of obscurity and ironic self-importance—it matched the band's affect, and anti-bourgeois orientation to the late Soviet world

---

[3]In a 2012 interview for the online news site *Khaivei* (Highway), Zdorenko explained his sartorial choices in greater detail: "We were brave about our image. I performed in baggy stretch pants, lacquered boots, a jacket for a T-shirt, and my father's proletarian beret. It was like an image of an alcoholic, who in the mornings would go out to get drunk with his tote bag."

[4]"Ve-Ve" should sound like the first two letters of the English word "very." After 1989, the band substituted the Ukrainian word "volannia" for the Russian word "vopli" in their band name, but on the occasions where their full band name is used—rather than the much more common abbreviation of VV—it seems that most people continue to use the Russian "vopli."

Figure 1.2 *VV in 1988 as depicted in* Fonohraf. *From the personal archives of O. Rudiachenko. Used with permission.*

in which they formed. This world was ruled by a political class that had declared war against Western popular music for its "dangerous ideological pollution among Soviet youth."[5] It was a world in which Soviet ideologues of the "disco mafia" produced rubrics to "organize ideologically reliable dance parties" in an effort to tamp down on corrupting influences from the West.[6] In this world, VV mockingly raised the stakes—*ok fine, we will dance, but we will do it in our ungovernable way.*

---

[5]These were Yuri Andropov's words, published in *Pravda* on July 15, 1983, cited in Sergei Zhuk, "'The Disco Mafia' and 'Komsomol Capitalism' in Soviet Ukraine During Late Socialism," in *Material Culture in Russia and the USSR* (Routledge, 2020), 149. There were earlier chapters in the conflict between Soviet officialdom and rock music. Boris Schwarz reminds of how, in August 1968, "a group of young Ukrainians defied the music curbs by writing an open letter to *Pravda Ukrainy,* the official Communist newspaper, protesting against the paper's backward and conservative attitude towards young people's cultural tastes, "In our country people go almost into hysterics when they see a young man with hair á la Beatles, and with a guitar as well" (Schwarz 1972, 491).
[6]Ibid., 148.

VV coalesced in 1986: bassist Pipa and guitarist Zdorenko had started playing hard rock together in a band called SOS in 1981 and were searching for a lead guitarist. Instead, they found Skrypka, a bayan (button accordion) and saxophone player, who came on board and quickly became the charismatic front man and primary lyricist for the group. Serhiy Sakhno, who grew up in Chernobyl and trained at a music school (музучилище) as a conductor, joined as the group's drummer in 1987. Skrypka told me that, although "there were other groups using bayan in rock bands at the time, no one else played it like a rock instrument."[7] This approach led the group to innovate what has often been called Ukrainian "ethno-punk." In 1987, they were among the first Soviet Ukrainian bands to write lyrics in Ukrainian rather than Russian, milking the ironic and subversive potentials of a language that had been suppressed and often denigrated as a kind of hillbilly dialect throughout the Soviet twentieth century. (Their often-ambiguous applications of language invited controversy as to whether VV intended to further mock the Ukrainian language or position it into a place of privilege, a tension I explore in detail in Chapter three.)

Despite being latecomers to the Kyiv rock scene, by the end of 1987, VV became one of its most prominent bands, and one of a few driving forces steering the culture of that rock scene away from heavy metal and towards punk. By late 1988, with the release of the music video for "Tantsi"—the first Ukrainian music video ever made—they had been named the "Soviet rock group of the year" by Artemy Troitsky, the Soviet rock critic whose presence on television gave visibility and legitimacy to late Soviet youth musical subcultures. The cassette album of *Tantsi* in 1989 further burnished their popularity, helping to

---

[7]Personal interview, April 15, 2019.

rocket them to fame across the expanse of the USSR, and making them the first Soviet Ukrainian group to find enthusiastic audiences in Western Europe (especially in France).

I don't remember the particulars, but I first heard a bootleg of *Tantsi* in the early 2000s, when a Ukrainian friend—astonished at how little I knew of Ukrainian popular music—burned an MP3 CD of essential listening to kickstart my musical education. The song "Tantsi" instantly seduced me. It was probably a decade or more later, long after the song had lodged itself firmly in my ears, that I went in pursuit of the irresistible beat again. By then, the video had been uploaded to YouTube, and I watched it on loop. "Tantsi," for me, became a noisy meditation, a blast of late Soviet Ukrainian punk confetti into otherwise monochrome moments of annotating bibliographies in preparation for my graduate exams or slogging through the latest book of lofty academic theory. Bam! Ta-ta-ta-tantsi.

To be consumed by a song was not unusual for me. But my fascination with "Tantsi" was different from those other songs that I had once obsessively loved (rewinding as soon as it ended; the small thrill of anticipation before it started again). Like many Americans reared on Reaganite Cold War rhetoric, my image of the USSR was of a stolid and rather sexless place. This image was bolstered by my family's story of arrival in North America as post-WWII displaced persons, refugees from Soviet power. Contemporary Ukraine seemed to me thoroughly Sovietized, somehow less "authentic" than the version of Ukraine our émigré community hoped to restore one day.[8] In the Ukrainian-American

---

[8] In her 2001 book *The Future of Nostalgia*, Svetlana Boym makes a useful distinction between "restorative" and "reflective" nostalgias. Restorative nostalgia "attempts a transhistorical reconstruction of the lost home," and matches my experience of being raised Ukrainian in the US diaspora (2001, xviii).

enclaves, my childhood had been populated by stories of freedom fighting warriors on horseback, of folkloric girls in flower crowns, of our nineteenth-century poet-hero Shevchenko's patriotic exhortations. At Ukrainian-American gatherings, we mourned Stalinist mass death, and took satisfaction in knowing that we weren't the ones living in the "evil empire." In Ukrainian scouting camps, we sang songs about how we children of the diaspora would one day "defend Ukraine from enemy hands"—a lyric that admittedly took on shocking new meaning following the full-scale Russian invasion of Ukraine in February 2022. All of this diasporic culture confirmed to me that the Ukrainians *over there* were different from the Ukrainians *over here*. The fact that "Tantsi" was made by such irreverent, kinetic, *familiar* people, so distant from my alternately lachrymose and romantic ideas of Ukraine, was destabilizing to the comforting contrast: monochrome there, technicolor here.

And so it was this punk quartet, with one weird song about dancing, that cast many of those baseline certainties into question. Like a message in a bottle sent from the late Soviet past, "Tantsi" suggested that there was more to the simple, reassuring morality tales of diaspora life. The song suggested new ways to connect to my heritage, ways that did not rest exclusively on nostalgia and nationalism. The song opened a portal to a Kyiv that *must* have been a vibrant scene of late Soviet musical creation: evidence that young people there had been experimenting, partying, dancing all along.

Although my teenage encounter with "Tantsi" may have been naive, its impact on me was—I subsequently learned—not unique. Nor was the portal it opened in my own life confined to the context of a politicized diaspora. Even in its own late-1980s Kyiv context—according to Zhenya Rohachevsky, who took over as lead guitarist in the band after Zdorenko left in 1993—VV's punk rock amounted to "a revolution." He described hearing them as an "explosion," a "cultural phenomenon" with a singular impact in the late Soviet rock scene. Rohachevsky was sixteen years old when he first heard the song "Tantsi" on the Radiotochka (Радіоточка), the Soviet radio transmitted throughout the USSR via devices wired into the walls. The song played on the radio in the evening and fostered in him what he described in 2019 as "cognitive dissonance," since he was hearing it on the same device that was widely referred to as "the liar" (брехунець) for broadcasting party propaganda.[9] To hear "Tantsi," and in the Ukrainian language—ironic, subversive, but still viscerally inspiring—played on the Radiotochka was itself a "rupture." He thinks it must have been 1989 by the time he heard the song. Before Gorbachev's reforms of the mid-1980s—*uskorennia* (acceleration), *perebudova* (restructuring), *glasnost* (openness), and democratization—he believes that no one could have imagined hearing anything like this on the radio. He described perceiving the song on multiple levels: musical, subcultural, and psychological, akin to the "psychodramas of Dostoevsky." Sitting on the sidewalk of the Vagabond Café in Kyiv in May 2019, thirty years later, he told me: "I fell in love immediately and forever."

Eugene Hütz, best known as the front man of the "Gypsy punk" band Gogol Bordello, came of age in the Kyiv punk scene, and described being "overtaken with a sense of wonder" upon hearing VV for the first time.

---

[9]In the late 1980s, Andriy Panchyshyn, a singer in the cabaret-musical group Не Журись (Don't Worry), wrote a song titled "The Liar" (*Брехунець*) dedicated to the state-controlled radio. In it, Panchyshyn sings: "Lying from birth/The end has come/My Soviet kitchen radio/Chokes on the truth." These translated lyrics appear in Adriana Helbig, "Ukraine," in *The International Recording Industries*, ed. Lee Marshall. (London: Routledge, 2013), 195.

When they started playing, it really hit me, like *this is it*, you know? That, finally, things are going to the next level. This whole metal, blues-punk, blues-alternative music plus ethnic music, it was an amalgamation. *That's* the hybrid. *That's* the fucking vitamins I need. I went completely H.A.M.[10] After that, I didn't miss one show of VV until I left [for the US] in 1990, including smaller shows in small theaters that were almost acoustic, including their show on the Andriivski Spusk,[11] including their show with Sonic Youth.

Reminiscing on his years as a superfan of the Kyiv punk scene, Hütz told me, "Perhaps I have the advantage of enjoying a very unique perspective on this whole creation of VV, because I was, in a way, a fly on the wall. I was younger than everybody by like five years, and no one was taking me seriously. I was just like a punk guy who was going to do like production assistance, or whatever. But I was there in the mix . . . " He described himself, along with his friend Ivan Derbastler (now a prominent DJ), as "guys on the fly"—unofficial runners, on standby to help out in any way:

If Sashko Pipa forgot his bass, we were sent across town to get the bass, things like that. And we would consider it to be a very special mission. I remember bringing the bass on the subway, without the case. Pipa had that super eccentric square bass that he made out of I don't know what—some, like, old furniture [laughs], I don't know. I remember standing

---

[10]A slang acronym for "hard as a motherfucker."
[11]Andriivski Spusk, or (in Ukrainian) Andriivski Uzviz, is a famous serpentine street in central Kyiv. It is a key artery that connects the oldest neighborhood in the city, Podil, to its monumental center.

in the packed subway during rush hour with this bass on my shoulder, and I was like fifteen, and people were looking at me like, "what the fuck is this snow shovel for?" And I was looking around like, you guys have no idea how incredible this sacramental object is that I'm carrying, actually. And how just within an hour and a half, you know, several hundred people who are part of this punk rock cult are going to go completely H.A.M. to the sounds of this snow shovel.[12]

Today, Hütz remains steadfast in his belief that VV's *Tantsi* amounted to a tectonic shift. He described how "VV had a distinctly Kyivan vibe, this hip Kyiv vibe. It was something about their body language, they had that Kyiv swag." In Hütz's view, the local spin that VV put on punk rock made a "positive statement on behalf of Ukrainian culture." Needless to say, VV also deeply influenced the aesthetics of Gogol Bordello, the band that Hütz formed on the Lower East Side of Manhattan in 1999 and led to international notoriety in the 2000s.

Apparently, Jello Biafra, the front man of the Dead Kennedys, called VV the "best Soviet punk rock band."[13] Contemporaneous *samizdat* publications and official Soviet music magazines both attested to the revolutionary nature of the band's 1989 *Tantsi* cassette release, which contained fourteen tracks, mostly recorded in one frenetic night. Even today, the multiple Facebook groups, thriving blogosphere, and other online groups dedicated to VV's early years testify to the enduring appeal of the eponymous hit song and the album, which

---

[12]Personal interview, February 3, 2022.
[13]Numerous people repeated this to me, though I have not been able to find it in any written account.

introduced listeners to several songs that later iterations of VV would re-record and release on their official post-Soviet albums. In 1989, the album *Tantsi* circulated through a new tape-dubbing enterprise named *Fonohraf*, which began its life as a cooperative founded by the Kyivan music editor Oleksandr Rudiachenko in 1989.[14] The album never had an official release: until now, with the remastered vinyl offering from Org Music, paired to the publication of this short book, and which I have had the privilege to shepherd into existence in collaboration with the original band members and a US-based team of audio engineers. (More on this at the end of the book.)

Not everyone agrees, however, that *Tantsi* merits a book in its honor. Oleksandr Rudiachenko, the respected Kyiv-based music journalist who was responsible for the cassette's release through *Fonohraf* in 1989, told me that he would not have chosen to present this particular artifact to Anglophone readers. He would have opted for something more official and canonical (such as Taras Petrynenko and Hrono's album *I am a Professional Slave*, released though the Ukrainian-Canadian joint enterprise "Kobza" in 1989), or something more respectable and current (such as Onuka's excellent 2014 debut record, *Onuka*).[15] Oleg Skrypka told me repeatedly that the band does not acknowledge the 1989 *Tantsi* album as an official VV release, but rather as a demo tape (though he gave his permission for its digitization and re-mastering in conjunction

---

[14]The tape-dubbing enterprise "Fonohraf" shares the name, and included some of the same personnel, as the "Fonohraf" music pages of the Communist Youth League newspaper. The reason for this is more clearly explained in the following chapter.
[15]Personal interview, January 5, 2022.

with this book).[16] I myself confess to small pangs of desire when I consider the many deserving Ukrainian albums that I could have chosen to write about instead of *Tantsi*—from the astonishing 1976 album of Ukrainian traditional songs by the trio "Golden Keys" (Золоті Ключі); to the albums of VV's contemporaries Vika Vradiy (crowned "Miss Rock Europe" in 1992) or The Snake Brothers (Брати Гадюкіни); to the experimental jazz-folk recordings of Mariana Sadovska; to world music darlings DakhaBrakha's 2010 album *Light*; to the rapper Alyona Alyona's 2019 *Pushka*. There are others. But *Tantsi* still stands out, because aside from my personal love for the songs on VV's *Tantsi*—rough edges included—this album allows me to unspool a story that includes but also exceeds the aesthetic domain, opening into themes about how 1980s sound recording technologies, Soviet TV and radio infrastructures, shifting cultures of celebrity, censorship, protest, entrepreneurialism, linguistic politics, and the expressive potentials of punk rock converged during the volatile *perestroika* years to produce an artifact as bizarre, provocative, and delightful as *Tantsi*.

This book therefore considers *Tantsi*—the 1989 cassette release by a band of legendary status in Ukraine and beyond— as a paradigmatic example of how messy things got in Gorbachev's USSR. I will explore how distinctions between official and unofficial cultural production became increasingly blurred as Soviet citizens were granted new entrepreneurial freedoms, and how brazen young people became about

---

[16]Diehard fans will know that VV went on to make studio recordings of nearly all the songs on the 1989 cassette release, starting with the Kobza studio recordings made in late 1989, and extending into albums recorded well into the twenty-first century.

making the music they wanted to hear, apparatchiks be damned. My focus will be limited to the years between 1986 (when VV formed) and 1989 (the year of the album's release).[17] A celebrated example of a Soviet *magnitoalbom* (магнитоальбом), the cassette itself participated in an emergent semi-formal economy, outside of the monopoly of the official Soviet record label *Melodiya*, but also free of any infrastructural support typically associated with record labels. The story of *Tantsi* traverses a time of ideological whiplash when entrenched Soviet norms were rapidly exchanged for new ones, when ad hoc infrastructures rose and fell to meet the demands of burgeoning musical subcultures, when the paradoxical nature of life in what would become the last years of the USSR inspired young people to seek out new ways of living and new horizons of possibility. Drawing on original documents from the period, the vast digital archives created by VV fans, and interviews with original band members, journalists, and fans who were there at the time, I document how, in the late 1980s, recordings such as *Tantsi* were traded by fans through nascent tape-dubbing cooperatives such as *Fonohraf*, activating networks of late Soviet citizens who found each other at spaces on the margins of mainstream Soviet society—and in doing so, created new social worlds. As a

---

[17]VV is still prominent in Ukraine today. Oleg Skrypka and the drummer Serhiy Sakhno are the only two players from the original lineup who remain in the band. Yuri Zdorenko left the band in 1993, and Sashko Pipa remained until 2006. Both have, in public interviews, cited aesthetic differences as well as disputes around ownership for songs written before intellectual property protections existed in Ukraine. Pipa and Zdorenko formed the band "Borshch" (Борщ) in 2002 and continued to perform in a variety of projects until the full-scale invasion of Ukraine in February 2022, when Pipa turned towards territorial defense. Skrypka is today a prominent figure in the Ukrainian culture industries, known for creating the *etno-muzyka* festival "Kraina Mriy" (Dreamland), and actively touring in support of the Ukrainian war effort in 2022.

latecomer and outsider to this scene—I was born in 1981 in the US, not in Ukraine in the 1960s or 1970s—I hope to revive something of what this vivid scene must have looked like to its members, as opposed to the monochrome shades of my childhood imagination.

In 2019, lead singer Oleg Skrypka described the Soviet 1980s to me in the following way: "The world was paradoxical. We simply showed this absurdity." Created from within the strictures and infrastructures that governed, enabled, and often constrained Soviet musical life, the paradoxes thematized in *Iantsi* undermined Soviet officialdom in two ways: by weaving in and out of approved channels as was convenient, and by mocking Soviet hypocrisy through absurdly subversive uses of sound and poetry. Revisiting the anthropologist Alexei Yurchak's influential idea of how late Soviet discourse became "hypernormalized"—that is, in which the meanings of official Soviet discourse became almost entirely unmoored from their original intended uses, making them ripe for resignification—I analyze *Tantsi* as an artifact that advances a critique of authoritative state apparatuses through the strategic use of hypernormalized poetic and visual tropes (the iconic ТАНЦІ banner is one example). When blended with vernacular Ukrainian linguistic strategies of irony, the absurdist pleasures of the album are further intensified. Tracing this one album also allows a grounded vantage on the unstable terrain of the *perestroika* era, when, as Tatyana Yezhova, the editor of the Kyiv *samizdat* publication *Huchnomovets* told me, "Everything was changing fast." Yezhova recounted how norms could change on a monthly or even weekly basis: standards of censorship loosened or tightened, festivals allowed greater or lesser freedom from Komsomol oversight, rock groups were given greater or lesser leeway to tour. This unpredictable flux of late Soviet life encouraged inventive young people to dance their way around capricious barriers.

The example of *Tantsi* joins many works that have sought to nuance the easy Cold War narrative that posits a direct link between youth rock subcultures and the fall of the USSR. The stories I tell show how punk rock could exist in oblique relationship to state power, rumbling through its foundations in pursuit of new horizons of fun and freedom. Unlike the saccharine pop sanctioned by the Soviet state *(estrada)*, punk musicians adapted ideologies of rock to roast the absurdities of Soviet life and to celebrate the cathartic pleasures of collective gatherings organized around musical performances. In doing so, they fostered Soviet youth communities that existed in shifting and sometimes shadowy relation to state control–often ignoring the system rather than outrightly resisting it. VV's *Tantsi* exemplifies how Soviet musical cultures existed within an ecosystem of contradictions as entrenched state infrastructures collided with emergent youth subcultures on the quicksand of late Soviet life.

Such themes are likely familiar to those who have followed the writing that has attempted to nuance our views of late Soviet culture. What this book adds is the perspective from Kyiv, Ukraine, where the question of (an often ambiguous) language politics plays a consequential role for the trail VV blazed into the post-Soviet era. Additionally, this book tests out ideas about how to place Kyiv on the map of Soviet youth subcultures: was it peripheral, or core? Generations of scholars have grappled with the question of Ukraine's status as a postcolony; this book explores how one cohort of late Soviet citizens viewed themselves as variously inside or outside of the Soviet core. Finally, this book also seeks to examine how a seemingly ephemeral artifact of late Soviet culture—a quickly recorded demo tape from 1989—continues to provoke many of us to dance through the absurdities of everyday life.

The Making of *Tantsi*

The 1989 cassette album of *Tantsi* included fourteen tracks, running at a playtime of approximately forty-five minutes. Nine tracks are sung in Ukrainian, the remaining five are in Russian. Thirteen of the tracks—*Tantsi* ("Dances"), *Ia Letel* ("I Flew"), *Olia*, *Kruk oviak-Rock*, *Tovarysh Maior* ("Comrade Major"), *Politrok*, *Polonyna* ("Mountain Meadow"), *Buly Den'ki* ("There Were Days"), *Muzika*, *Rassvet* ("Dawn"), *Naliahai* ("Press On"), *Kolyskova* ("Lullaby"), and *Hey! Liubo!* ("Hey! O.K.!")—were recorded in one night, at a DIY session that took place at the Kurdiumova Institute of Metallurgy (Металофізики) in a neighborhood called Akademmistechko, located on the western periphery of Kyiv.[18] In 2019, I met Sashko Pipa, the original bassist, in Akademmistechko. Akademmistechko is an "urban massif" (масив) designed and built in the 1960s to house Kyiv-based scholars and scientists who could live near the various scholarly research institutes that were also included in the neighborhood plan. It is the neighborhood where Pipa and Zdorenko, the children of workers at the scientific institutes, grew up. We walked past the Institute of Metallurgy, and Pipa pointed out the area where they used to rehearse. Eventually, we settled into a spot on the sunny terrace of a local restaurant, where Pipa shared that he had the original master tape—a BASF reel-to-reel

---

[18]Two of the Russian-language songs—"Ia Letel" and "Rassvet"—had appeared on VV's first lesser-known *magnitoalbom*, "Aiaiaiaiaiaiaiai," recorded in 1987. The liner notes for the Org Music reissue of *Tantsi* contain translations of the lyrics and information on each song.

tape imported from Germany—from the 1989 session in his possession. He then described the session that resulted in that master tape:

> Back then, it was not like in the civilized world, where a band could pay to go into a rehearsal studio to rehearse—there was nothing like that. For a group to exist, to have rehearsals, you had to settle in somewhere (влаштуватися кудись). This was called "amateur art" (художня самодіяльність). Every enterprise—every depot, institute, school—all had a department of culture, and they would usually have drums and amplifiers and things like that somewhere. It was a whole art form to know how to align your group. And we aligned with a lot of places, but in particular with the Institute of Metallurgy ... So there was an assembly hall (актовий зал), a hall for small concerts and gatherings, and next to it there was a little room where we could rehearse. To record yourself in a real studio at that time was basically impossible. There were some real studios in the underground, but they were elsewhere—they were very expensive, or in Russia. And real professional studios were under the control of the state, so to be recorded, you needed the permission of the state, and for us this was just unrealistic. And so, this is why we decided to record ourselves. We borrowed a reel-to-reel tape recorder, a Soviet one—it was called "Elektronika-002." ... Back then in Kyiv there was a cult group called "Kollezhskyi Asessor" (Collegiate Assessor), very cool.[19] Their bass guitarist [Sashko Kyevtsev] was also studying at the Kyiv Polytechnic, in the Faculty of Acoustics; he knew a little more than we did about

---

[19]This cult alternative rock band's name refers to the lowest rank of bureaucrats in Imperial Russia. The musicians started playing together in Kyiv in 1981 and settled on this name in 1988.

sound recording. So we asked him to come and help, so he came and managed the process . . .

So we set up the drums in the little concert hall. And I still like the sound of the drums on that recording. I am the author of this sound [laughs]. I put the Soviet microphones in front of the drums. And the rest of us sat in the neighboring room, the three of us. So we played and recorded all of it without overdubs, all together, absolutely live. Live in stereo. And practically all the songs were maximum maybe second takes, and some of them were first takes. Back then we were playing practically every day, training, playing well—and most importantly, we believed we were the best band in the world [laughs]. That's why it all came out very nicely for us. We were very self-confident. There was no second-guessing. And that's how we recorded—"yeah, beautiful, lovely"—and that was that, it was recorded. When we took a second take, we would erase the first take and record over it. And that's how in one evening, in two or three hours, we recorded the whole thing.

The fourteenth song that made it onto the cassette album, "Mahatma," was added to the sequence later and taken from a live performance at the Institute of Foreign Languages. The master tape also contained at least eleven additional tracks that were left on the cutting room floor, some of which made it into VV's later repertoire. Songs that were popular in the 1980s were recorded but not included on the cassette. This included "Pisen'ka" (Пісенька, or Little Song), VV's first hit song.[20] And the VV song now known as

---

[20]In an October 2021 interview for *Telegid*, Oleg Skrypka boasted that "Pisen'ka" started VV on their "path to fame" and "formed the spirit of the Ukrainian underground." https://tinyurl.com/29edahvj, accessed January 2022.

Figure 1.3 Fonohraf *advertisement for the "Tantsi" cassette release in* Moloda Gvardia. *From the personal archives of O. Rudiachenko. Used with permission.*

"Laznia" (Лазня), officially released in the Ukrainian language in 2019, was there, in embryonic form and in the Russian language under the name "Banya" (Банька).

After deciding which tracks to include on the cassette for *Fonohraf*, the band members sequenced the original cassette by re-recording it with two microphones. On March 29, 1989, it was advertised to Kyivan *melomany* (music fans) in the pages of the local Komsomol newspaper *Moloda Gvardia*, with instructions on where to go to obtain a copy of the cassette tape in the newly established *Fonohraf* cooperative space. The newspaper included the black and white cover art for the cassette—designed by the music journalist Oleksandr Yevtushenko, who was one of the group's major early champions—with an image of scissors and a dotted line for listeners to cut to the correct dimensions (see Figure 1.3).

Stylistically, the early songs of VV, captured on the 1989 cassette album, are all over the place. In the first known mainstream journalistic feature on the group, published in *Moloda Gvardia* on July 20, 1988, Oleksandr Yevtushenko described their sound as follows: "To be precise in questions of style, VV has achieved a unique alloy of folklore, punk rock, and pop music. They do not do so without kitsch, which in VV's version is very reminiscent of the realities of life in the suburbs. An openness to life, emotional and spiritual emancipation— these the are the positive charges that drive the sharpest hit songs of this team." (I read Yevtushenko's last sentence here, printed in the official Komsomol newspaper, as participating in the same bloated rhetorical strategies of late Soviet irony that are typical in VV's lyrics.) In his 2011 book *Україна IN ROCK*, Yevtushenko repeatedly refers to VV as a "crazy turbo-punk-machine" (шалена турбо-панк-машина).[21] To Kyrylo Stetsenko, a prominent musician of the 1960s wave of Ukrainian rock, their style was "theatrical post-punk," which put on grotesque display the schizophrenic nature of life in the last years of the USSR.[22] In the 2016 documentary "Crank the Sound, Please!" (Дайте Звук, Будь Ласка!), the Ukrainian musical impresario known as Mokh (Oleg Gnativ) describes his first impression of VV as "like a hurricane," and asserts, "I always said and still say that VV are the Ukrainian Sex Pistols."[23]

---

[21]Oleksandr M. Yevtushenko, *Ukraïna IN ROCK*, De Profundis (Kyiv: Hrani-T, 2011), 52, 68.

[22]Personal interview, January 2, 2022.

[23]VV never shared the stage with the Sex Pistols, but they did play with Sonic Youth when they came to Kyiv as part of the "International Rock Bridge" (Интер-Рок-Мост) festival on April 14, 1988. The documentary referenced here was released on YouTube in two parts in 2016 and 2017 by "Huchnomovets Productions with the participation of Gippos Video Studio." It focuses on Kyivan rock music between the years of 1986 and 1995. Part one can be viewed at https://www.youtube.com/watch?v=K6QycrwD2EE. Mokh is interviewed about VV at 37 minutes.

Skrypka has referred to VV's style at the time as "late socialist realism, with elements of cubism," embracing an "intentional simplicity" apparent in songs such as "Muzika," "Politrok," and others.[24] His teenage interest in the blues is audible on numerous tracks through bluesy riffs rendered on his bayan. In the first known interview with the members of VV, published in the second issue of the Kyiv *samizdat Subjecticon* in early 1988, Pipa is quoted as saying that "We deny the music of the 80s and are interested in the music of the 60s"—though elsewhere in the same interview the band members declare that they are all listening to more contemporary acts: the German New Wave band Trio, the British ska band Madness, and the Soviet Russian pop singer Nina Nenavesha.[25] In 2019, Pipa underscored the influence that Soviet state-sanctioned popular musics, *estrada*, had on the band's early output: "We listened to the worst Soviet *estrada* music, and imagined that it was punk. And it all mixed together, in the musical plan, and in the way we showed it on stage."[26] Zdorenko and Pipa's earlier stylistic experiments in heavy metal also peek through in the distorted guitar riffs and propulsive bass patterns that animate a number of songs.

In later chapters I will say more about the stylistic and lyrical elements of other songs on the album, but in this introductory chapter I return to "Tantsi," since it was and is one of VV's most beloved hits, performed at nearly every concert since the late 1980s, known today by generations of fans. "Tantsi" appears as

---

[24]Personal interview, June 5, 2019. See also: https://slukh.media/texts/tancy-story/.

[25]This interview was republished on Tatyana Yezhova's blog: https://lehautparleur.livejournal.com/80664.html.

[26]Personal interview, May 13, 2019.

the eponymous track of the 1989 cassette; in 1988, it was voted "Song of the Year" of the Kyiv rock scene, flooding the Kyiv underground with "Tantsi" buttons and agitprop-style banners made by VV's manager at the time, the sculptor Volodymyr Ivanov. The song came together in 1987, while Skrypka was working at a research and production association called "Quantum," and where he was held to a strict worker's regime: arriving at 8:00 a.m., leaving at 5:00 p.m. Inspiration struck during his lunch break. This mundane workplace experience is reflected in the lyrics, where he establishes, in the first verse, that "the workers are tired of working." The second verse imagines a typical Soviet worker's thoughts in such robotic terms that it suggests an over-the-top caricature of the *homo sovieticus*: "We recollect all week / There is much chatter and many opinions / We wait until good Sunday comes / The dance hall invites us / In the club there were lovely dances / Happy, good, good dances." Skrypka told me that, when they performed "Tantsi" live for the first time at a venue colloquially known as "Hollywood," they put it in the middle of the set. "And it was just like a grenade had exploded in the hall." He explained that "when you write a song, you don't know whether it's a hit or not a hit, you don't know. And when we played it in the middle of the concert, people just—they were lying on the stage, screaming, behaving like animals. And we understood it was a hit, and then in the next concert, the next day, we played it at the end of the set, understanding it was *our* hit."

From its start as a local favorite in Kyiv, "Tantsi" went on to Soviet-wide acclaim, largely because of the black and white music video described in the opening of this chapter, which was produced for Ukrainian State Television (УТ-1) and first shown on a monthly program called "Musical Video Mill" (Музичний Відеомлин), hosted by Kyrylo Stetsenko, in early

1989.[27] It was later shown on the Union-wide television program "The View" (Взгляд) and then "Program A" (Программа А), where it was introduced by the authoritative rock critic Artemy Troitsky. In early 2022, I conducted interviews with Kyrylo Stetsenko and the television editor who facilitated the making of the video, Elena Prigova, about how it came into existence. The story I retell below is a composite picture based on their recollections and those of other interviewees; not all of their memories were consistent, so I have done my best to triangulate between personal stories and written records.

Stetsenko told me that it was his idea to make a video featuring VV for his program; he was always hunting for segments to feature on the popular "Video Mill" television program, and he had been attending concerts at the newly established Kyiv Rock Club as part of his work as a radio journalist. Prigova recalled attending a show with Stetsenko, where they were both impressed by the audacious punk group who were a favorite of the young music heads. Stetsenko set out to persuade the band to make a video, recalling a couple of meetings with Pipa and Zdorenko that took place outdoors. The meetings, in Stetsenko's memory, were neither "super constructive" nor "concrete," but eventually the band agreed to participate in the making of what would become Ukraine's first music video. Prigova, as one of the youngest editors working at the television station, supported the endeavor and, together with the technical director of the video, Maryna Bohatykh, scheduled the time for filming.

---

[27] I have not been able to confirm exact dates for when the video was made and shown on television, but the timeline suggests that the video became a sensation *before* the *Tantsi* cassette began to circulate in late March of 1989, and so it was likely shown in January, February, or early March of 1989.

The video was filmed in a pavilion at the Ukr-telefilm studio on the Left-bank of Kyiv. Stetsenko recalled the agitprop terms drawn onto the side of massive buildings in the neighborhood near the studio: "Lenin," "Labor" (Труд), "May" (Май). When they entered the studio, which had been set up for another shoot as a bare white space with full lighting, Prigova and the technical director of the video, Maryna Bohatykh, agreed with Stetsenko that the setting was ideal: the video should focus on the charismatic young musicians, their strange facial expressions and bodily movements, with minimal distraction. But with one exception: the agitprop banner. But who would hold it? Luckily, workers in the pavilion next door were hammering away, and when Stetsenko went to plead with them to keep it quiet during filming, he realized they were the perfect extras for the film. Bribing them with a half-liter of vodka, the workers agreed to hold the ТАНЦІ banner in the shoot, never changing out of their blue worker's smocks. The shoot was efficient, only a couple of hours, and then Prigova and Bohatykh took the footage to the editing room. Stetsenko, who fretted over the process, was happy when he finally saw the minimalist result of their efforts.

Aware that the satirical nature of the music video could provoke Soviet censors to condemn it, Prigova then mounted what Stetsenko called a "political defense" of their creation. They called a focus group of three experts to analyze the video and give it sanction. The group included Taras Petrynenko, a star of Ukrainian popular music, Dmytro Pavlychko, a prominent musicologist, and Ivan Dziuba, a recently rehabilitated dissident and literary expert best known for authoring the banned book *Internationalism or Russification?* (1965), and leading protests against the Russification of Ukrainian with fellow dissidents, including the poet Vasyl Stus. Each offered their comments on "Tantsi" and explained why it was valuable. Dziuba, according to Prigova, offered the most insightful comments. Dziuba was a known defender of youth culture, having argued in the journal *Science and Culture (Наука і Культура)* in 1988 that:

> The full functioning of a national culture also requires the development of mass entertainment genres and forms, such as various types of cabaret, circus performance, happening, entertainment cinema, popular songs, and so on—that is, of youth subculture and urban subculture in general.[28]

Dziuba apparently argued that "Tantsi" needed to be shown in order to "cleanse" Ukrainian culture of its demons—his belief was that the grotesque and ironic display of VV would accelerate the exorcism. Nonetheless, after it aired, Prigova received an official reprimand (догана) for "jeering at the Ukrainian language" (знущання з Української мови). In January 2022, Prigova remembered this reprimand proudly, considering it her "sacrifice on behalf of Ukrainian culture."

Prigova then personally transported the film reel of the music video to Moscow, where she handed it to her close friend Nina Solovian, who was the main music editor for the popular Union-wide television program "The View" ("Згляд"). Prigova recalled "the visceral feeling on my skin at witnessing the shock of the people in Moscow, who did not speak Ukrainian," as they first viewed the video. They then showed it

---

[28]Cited in Romana Bahry, "The Satirical Current in Popular Youth Culture: Rock Music and Film in Ukraine in the 1990s" (paper presented in Ukraine in the 1990s: Proceedings of the First Conference of the Ukrainian Studies Association of Monash University, Monash University, 24–26 January 1992), 148.

on the television "on repeat." By that afternoon, she recalled, she heard people in the hallways of the Moscow television station repeating the phrase—"In the club there were lovely dances" (У клубі були любі танці)—mimicking Skrypka's rather strange Ukrainian pronunciation (January 10, 2022). According to Skrypka, after it was shown once on Union-wide television, "the entire Soviet Union exploded ... Our journey as stars in the USSR began with this video."[29]

The making of *Tantsi*—the album and the video—happened at a time when new openness in official Soviet media, the lessening threat of severe consequences for sneering at Soviet power, and shifting winds in the political economy converged. The making of *Tantsi* was therefore also about the making of new horizons of possibility for Soviet youth, as they simply made the music they wanted to hear.

What Was *Tantsi* and What Comes Next?

The following three chapters of this book put *Tantsi* into context: socially, linguistically, ideologically, and nostalgically. Chapter two explores the "tusovka"—the social circle, the roving party, or "the hang"—of Kyiv in the late 1980s, and the various infrastructures that supported it. Drawing on first-hand accounts of what it was like to acquire recordings, listen together, and attend shows, I map out networks of musicians and fans who formed the Kyiv rock scene, and position VV at its center. I engage Alexei Yurchak's influential idea of being *vnye*

---

[29]As quoted in https://tsn.ua/special-projects/oldstars/, accessed January 17, 2021.

("a position of that was simultaneously inside and outside of the rhetorical field of discourse, neither simply in support nor simply in opposition ... [therefore] becoming a dynamic Glavlit site where new meanings were produced")[30] to examine how late Soviet rock musicians and fans—who considered themselves *neformaly*, or nonconformists—contributed to a potent sense of community that emerged as an oblique, but nonetheless oppositional force, to Soviet power.

Chapter three, "Total *stiob*: Irony vs. hypocrisy" dives into the ambiguous and shifting representational and linguistic politics of VV, and their engagement with prominent archetypes of late Soviet Ukraine. I explore the aesthetics of late Soviet absurdity known as "stiob" and its connection to vernacular forms of Ukrainian humor, which the original band members insist added to the special success of VV in both Ukrainian and Russian rock scenes. I offer close analysis of the song "Buly Den'ki" to parse some of the polysemic potentials at work.

Chapter four, "Sex, drugs, and Komsomol," centers on the interaction between rockers and Komsomol apparatchiks. I write about strategies of control on the part of the state, and techniques of evasion and compromise used by bands such as VV. Focusing on the understudied rituals of lyrical censorship (*litovannia*: літовання (Ukr) / литование (Ru)) that rock musicians had to obey in the early months of *perestroika*, and the practices of auditioning for official status (*taryfikatsia*: тарифікація (Ukr)), this chapter shows how musicians navigated a period of volatile politics and shifting imperatives.

---

[30]Alexei Yurchak, *Everything Was Forever, Until It Was No More: The Last Soviet Generation* (Princeton, NJ: Princeton University Press, 2005), 288.

The book ends with a short conclusion reflecting on the afterlives of *Tantsi*. How does this object born from an anti-capitalist, non-Anglo-American network of music and media offer a unique perspective on music as a circulatory form that brings into being distinct modes of sociality? I end by contemplating what the first official release of *Tantsi*—remastered and issued three decades after *Tantsi* cassettes were first exchanged on the streets of Soviet Kyiv, now heard at a time of existential threat for Ukraine—might mean for the audiences who will hear this music anew, today.

2 *Tusovka*: Ad Hoc Infrastructures and the Kyiv Rock Scene

The June 5, 1991 issue of the *Moloda Gvardia* newspaper—advertised as the "socio-political publication of the Kyiv Regional Committee and the City Committee of the Komsomol"—featured an unusual map of the Kyiv Metro on the front of its music section. It is a map of a *tusovka*, an "enigmatic" slang term that the Russian rock journalist Artemy Troitsky defines as "The Scene," "The Big Mess," or "Something's Happening" in his 1990 book *Tusovka: Who's Who in the New Soviet Rock Culture*.[1] I often think of it as "The Hang." Titled "Schematic of Lines of the Kyiv Underground" (Схема Ліній Київського Андерграунда), the map featured the hammer and sickle insignia of the USSR on the top left of the page and renamed each stop on the Kyiv Metro with one of forty-odd rock bands of the late Soviet Kyivan rock *tusovka*. The Kyiv Metro, then as now, is comprised of three main intersecting lines (red, green, and blue). The triangle in the center of the map shows the three transfer stations: The Golden Gates/Leninska stations appear as Lost World/Apartment 50; Lev Tolstoy Plaza/Sports Palace are Er Jazz[2]/Kollezhskyi Asessor;

---

[1] A. Troitsky, *Tusovka : Who's Who in the New Soviet Rock Culture* (London and New York: Omnibus Press 1990).

[2] The name "Er Jazz" was short for "erotic jazz."

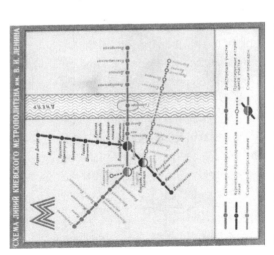

Figure 2.1 Map of the Kyiv Metro in 1989. Downloaded from starkiev.com/метро/схемы-линий

Figure 2.2 Yevtushenko's map of the "Kyiv Underground," published in Fonohraf in 1991. From the personal archives of O. Rudiachenko. Used with permission by O. Rudiachenko and O. Yevtushenko-Yakovleva.

and, at the very beating heart of the urban underground infrastructure, the October Revolution Square/Khreshchatyk stations, are the heavy metal band Edem (key players in the founding of the Komsomol-sponsored Kyiv Rock Club), and our theatrical post-punk darlings, VV.[3]

According to Oleksandr Rudiachenko, the editor of *Fonohraf*, this symbolic map was designed by the rock journalist Oleksandr Yevtushenko, and reflects, to some degree, that music journalist's subjective picture of how the key players of the rock scene fit in terms of genre and importance. Each metro line represents a genre trajectory prominent in the underground at the time—from the "new romantics" (Lost World), to the "hard rockers" (Apartment 50), to the "folk-punk" and "nationally conscious Ukrainian speaking groups" line (VV), to the "domestic metal" bands (Edem), to the mostly instrumental avant-garde (Er Jazz), to the indie bands (Kollezhskyi Asessor). The farther out the stop on the Metro, the less influential the band.[4] In this image, the durable infrastructure of the Soviet city is claimed as the terrain of upstart young musicians.

---

[3] I first became aware of this map through pure chance, when I visited Kyiv in October 2021, and struck up a conversation with a man selling re-prints of Soviet propaganda posters at the bottom of the Andriivskyi Uzviz in central Kyiv. We spoke at length about a different research project of mine (on Soviet children's music) and then he gifted me a burned CD of his late son's band, Frog in the Airship (Жаба в Дирижаблі), which included—in the booklet— a photocopy of this map from 1991. That band falls along the track that Rudiachenko identified as "theatrical punk shows," culminating in "a real crime in aesthetics—the real Lukyanivska prison" (January 17, 2022).

[4] Many of these Metro stops were renamed after Ukrainian Independence in 1991. "October Revolution Square," for example, became "Independence Square" (the central site of two significant post-Soviet revolutions). I am extremely grateful to Oleksandr Rudiachenko for helping me decode Yevtushenko's image.

But, superimposing the bands of the Kyivan "underground" rock scene onto a map of the city's underground infrastructure, the Metro, is not only a clever graphic pun. It is evidence of the urban network—robust and hierarchical, even if mediated through one important journalist's perspective—that existed at the time. Take note that this was published in early June of 1991, merely two-and-a-half months before the Ukrainian parliament declared its independence from the Soviet Union on August 24, 1991. That this snapshot of the Kyiv rock scene, the self-identified cultural "underground," appeared in the official Komsomol newspaper—a publication ostensibly in service of the Leninist youth still tasked with building the future of Communism—is a sign of the rapidly changing times. The comedic codes and irreverent inclusion of the state's loftiest symbols (the hammer and the sickle), demonstrate the way in which citizens contributed to the hollowing out of Soviet ideology in the last years of the USSR. It is suggestive of the many undergrounds of late Soviet Kyiv—of other, less permanent, infrastructures of the time.

This chapter considers the play between official, unofficial, and semi-official infrastructures in Kyiv in the late Soviet 1980s, demonstrating how various entities enabled the sociality and musical culture of Kyivan *neformaly* (nonconformist youth). I begin from the premise that, like any cultural product, *Tantsi* did not emerge in a vacuum.[5] It came into existence in the turbulent context of late Soviet Kyiv, where it was supported

---

[5]It is important to note, as well, that this moment in Ukrainian rock history had its historical precedent in the first wave of Ukrainian rock in the 1960s, defined by bands such as Taras Petrynenko and Kyrylo Stetsenko's "Enei" (Aeneas). Although I do not have space here to describe these precedents, Romana Bahry's valuable chapter in *Rocking the State* provides a useful overview, see Bahry, "Rock Culture and Rock Music in Ukraine."

(or, when convenient, ignored) by a patchwork of entities, some of them newly legal under evolving Gorbachevian reforms. Rather than attempt a comprehensive overview of the many media, audio, and performance infrastructures that existed and intersected at the time, this chapter centers on just four contrasting "sonic infrastructures" that helped to shape and reinforce the Kyiv underground scene.[6] I emphasize the ad hoc nature of these infrastructures, noting how they arose and morphed to meet the needs of music fans, concert organizers, and bands. In a climate of scarcity—when music fans often congregated in kitchens to listen to bootleg reel-to reel tapes after the bars and cafes closed at 9:00 or 10:00 pm, and when bands had to scrape together the resources to record on a four track with a handful of battered microphones—resourcefulness and ingenuity were hallmarks of all the ad hoc infrastructures that supported the scene.

The first infrastructure I consider is *Fonohraf*, which in truth consisted of two independent but related entities. *Fonohraf* began in 1985 as a column in the large-scale *Moloda Gvardia* (*Young Guard*) newspaper, and eventually expanded into a regular weekly music-focused insert in the paper. A second, related but independent enterprise also called *Fonohraf*, took advantage of the *perestroika* cooperative laws introduced in 1988 to expand into a legal commercial (if not particularly lucrative) enterprise. By 1989, these two *Fonohrafs*—purportedly independent but deeply interrelated—had morphed into something that was not quite a label, not quite

---

[6]Adam Kielman, "Sonic Infrastructures, Musical Circulation and Listening Practices in a Changing People's Republic of China," *Sound Studies* 4, no. 1 (2018).

a recording studio, not quite a PR company, not quite a venue, not quite a tape-dubbing distribution center, but had elements of all the above. What it offered, in any case, was a fleeting if critical infrastructure—grounded in its own ingenious circular economy—through which many albums of the late 1980s Kyiv rock scene became known and disseminated.

In addition to newly legal channels such as *Fonohraf* (in both its newspaper and tape-dubbing forms), unofficial *samizdat* publications championed and defined the musical underground: notable among these was the zine *Huchnomovets*, whose name, meaning "loudspeaker," was inspired by a lyric in the popular VV song "Pisen'ka" (Пісенька).

Third, a network of Komsomol-controlled rock clubs organized events in official venues, but usually with strings attached: at more restrictive times, lyrics were censored, and Komsomol leaders loomed, presiding over the rock proceedings in their formal attire. As policies on the democratization of commercial activity were introduced, alternative organizations sprang up to avoid some of these constraints. The important collective founded by Volodymyr Ivanov known as "Rock Artil" (Rock Guild),[7] in which VV joined two other influential bands, offered such an alternative to the short-lived and Komsomol-controlled Kyiv Rock Club. Another vital unofficial infrastructure was "Balka," the Kyivan black

---

[7]My translation of "Rock Artil" tries to capture some of the archaism present in the Ukrainian word "Artil." As Volodya Ivanov explained to me, they chose the word "Artil" in part because it sounded archaic, like the self-organized guilds of pre-modern artisans. The anachronistic term appealed to them because, back then, "anything archaic seemed anti-Soviet." I would note also that the nickname for the Kyiv Rock Club, *kuznia*, also references the archaic trade of blacksmithing.

market vinyl bazaar where the *neformaly* of Kyiv found each other amid the unsanctioned sounds of imported musics.[8]

Keying in on the ad hoc infrastructures of this scene reveals how individuals within the community of music fans of late Soviet Kyiv constructed their social worlds by moving between official, unofficial, and semi-official channels as was advantageous to their personal and collective desires and goals. I hope, through these examples, to offer a fresh perspective on the long-standing discussion of "being *vnye*" introduced by Alexei Yurchak in his influential 2005 book *Everything Was Forever, Until It Was No More*. In Yurchak's conception, being *vnye* meant refusing to participate in normative structures offered by the Soviet state, opting out of the entire system by not taking sides, participating in unofficial networks of exchange, and—in the case of musicians such as VV—using discursive techniques of irony and comedy to make artworks that were "socialist in form, indeterminate in content."[9] Kevin Platt and Benjamin Nathans, who attempted to historicize Yurchak's conception of being *vnye* by linking it to earlier generations of nonconformist literary expression and dissident activism, argued for greater consideration of how new "zones of individual autonomy" in the Thaw era that preceded Gorbachev's *perestroika* reforms "made possible the

---

[8]These infrastructures share much in common with the rock scenes in places such as Leningrad, where the official Rock Club was founded in 1981 (in Moscow the Rock Lab was opened in 1986). Several works published in the early 1990s have documented these scenes, including the works by Cushman, Ryback, Troitsky, and Chapter nine in Ramet, included in the bibliography. According to Ryback, it was the Tbilisi Rock Festival organized in part by Artemy Troitsky that "heralded the new era of Soviet rock and roll." In Ukraine, rock cultures did not become formally institutionalized until 1986.
[9]Kevin Platt and Benjamin Nathans, "Socialist in Form, Indeterminate in Content: The Ins and Outs of Late Soviet Culture," *Ab Imperio* (2011).

appearance of the movements for civil and human rights, the rise of environmental activism, a resurgence in ethnic nationalist thought, new tastes in music and fashion, and much more."[10] But the Soviet state's Thaw-era shift "from coercion and terror to collectivism and self-policing [as the] primary means of social control" exceeded the problem of individual autonomy that is spotlighted by Platt and Nathans. Overemphasizing individual agency risks a doubling down on the same liberal fantasy of individual freedom that Yurchak originally set out to critique. How, instead, did "being *vnye*" bear out in the lives of loosely constituted communities such as the Kyiv Rock *tusovka*? In that context, being *vnye* could mean acquiescing to certain official infrastructural demands but paying them little mind; or working within official infrastructures to obtain certain privileges, and then shifting tactics when new opportunities arose. *Perestroika*-era dynamics of public/ private played out not only for individuals, but for their friend groups and broader social networks—in this case, for the Kyiv Metro-sized constellation of bands mapped out by Yevtushenko in the pages of the Komsomol newspaper, for which VV was the North Star.

The Circular Economy of *Fonohraf*

Beginning on September 28, 1985, five months after Gorbachev first uttered the word *perestroika*, the Kyivan *Moloda Gvardia* newspaper started featuring a music section called *Fonohraf*. Edited by the visionary music critic Oleksandr Rudiachenko,

[10]Ibid., 312

and featuring the writing of the journalist Oleksandr Yevtushenko, it quickly gained a readership among Kyivan *melomany* ("music heads") thirsty for information on youth music cultures both local and distant. With its large circulation size—from 60,000 to 100,000 copies of each edition—*Fonohraf* covered the spectrum of contemporary music genres, from jazz to heavy-metal to punk.

Rudiachenko, who described his commitment to writing about rock and other underground musics as "a burden of pleasure," also told me at length about the "terrible musical hunger" in Kyiv at the time, about how fans would travel from the surrounding areas of Kyiv to pick up a fresh copy of *Moloda Gvardia* when *Fonohraf* appeared in the paper. At the beginning, Rudiachenko told me, "the term *rok-muzyka* was

Figure 2.3 *First printing of "U Koli Muz," announcing the scope of* Fonohraf. *From the personal archives of O. Rudiachenko. Used with permission.*

Figure 2.4 Fonohraf *logo. From the personal archives of O. Rudiachenko. Used with permission.*

not allowed," and he recalled going to the general editor weekly to discuss new euphemisms such as "youth music" (молодіжна музика). One editor, he told me, joked that their terminological inventiveness would "earn them a Nobel Prize."[11]

During its run from September 1985 through December of 1991, *Fonohraf* began to appear in the pages of *Moloda Gvardia*

---

[11]Personal interview, January 5, 2022.

with growing frequency, eventually developing into a weekly eight-column supplement to the newspaper, which provided a crucial stream of information for those interested in new bands, new releases, and local happenings. Rudiachenko described the overwhelming volume of fan letters—"kilograms of mail"—that began to pour in from ever-expanding geographic circles: first from within Kyiv, then its suburbs, then other regions of Ukraine, and eventually the Baltic and other Soviet republics. *Fonohraf* began to include hit parades, ranking based not on sales "because production, distribution, and copyright [were] not yet normalized: that is, there [were] as yet no laws governing these activities. Therefore they [were] based on telephone polls and letters to the newspaper."[12] In addition to responding to the desires of their readers, the writers at *Fonohraf* also served an archival function: the indispensable 1989 *Fonohraf Digest*, for example, attempted to historicize rock music in Ukraine by documenting various key acts and concerts going back to the 1960s across eighty pages of meticulous reporting. As a publication, *Fonohraf* became essential reading for Kyivan *neformaly* of all varieties: the metalheads, punks, hippies, jazzers, and anyone else attracted to music outside of the Soviet mainstream.

Oleksandr Yevtushenko, who would become one of post-Soviet Ukraine's most prominent rock critics, joined the staff of writers for *Fonohraf* after completing art school. He first wrote about Leningrad-based acts such as Akvarium, Kino, and Zoopark—many of whom became known outside the USSR following the release of the 1986 "Red Wave" album covertly smuggled out by Joanna Stingray—before realizing that the growing domestic Ukrainian scene deserved his attention.

---

[12]Bahry, "Rock Culture and Rock Music in Ukraine," 281.

Yevtushenko described the relative freedom of writing for *Moloda Gvardia*, since the newspaper was controlled not by the Communist Party at large but by its Youth League, the Komsomol, who were meant to cater to the tastes of young people. If censors complained that *Fonohraf* writers were advancing incorrect politics—as they did when Yevtushenko wrote a large spread on the first Ukrainian-language "Chervona Ruta" festival in 1989, perceived by Soviet power as a threatening hotbed of Ukrainian nationalist organizing—they could claim autonomy based on the editorial policies of the Komsomol youth who led the newspaper.[13] Rudiachenko told me that "if he was not reprimanded twice a year, he wasn't doing his job right." He recalled ludicrous meetings with censors where he tried to explain why a specific band was not "anti-Soviet"—that the German disco outfit Dschinghis Khan, with their insipid lyrics about Moscow's hot fire burning, was not actually advocating for dropping atomic bombs on the Kremlin, for example.[14] Protected somewhat by its official link to the Komsomol newspaper, *Fonohraf* was able to operate with not just a relatively high degree of autonomy, but also guaranteed funding. The Komsomol acted simultaneously as a shield and censor, at once bringing nonconformists under the umbrella of state power, while placing them in oblique relationship to its stakeholders.

---

[13]This story was recounted in an undated interview archived here: http://rock-oko.com/pro-avtora/ntervyu-karabas-lve.html (accessed May 7, 2021). Sadly, Yevtushenko passed in early 2020, and I was never able to interview him for this book. For more on the fraught politics of language and inclusion at the second "Chervona Ruta" festival, see Catherine Cowhey Wanner, *Burden of Dreams: History and Identity in Post-Soviet Ukraine*, Post-Communist Cultural Studies (University Park, PA: Pennsylvania State Univ. Press, 1998).
[14]Personal interview, January 5, 2022.

Soon, with new *perestroika* laws loosening restrictions on non-state commercial activity, Rudiachenko and like-minded cultural actors sought to expand the footprint of *Fonohraf* to better serve the various needs of Kyivan music fans. They eventually formed a cooperative, the "middle path between state socialism and free market individual capitalism" that recent economic reforms allowed.[15] *Fonohraf* therefore trailblazed many firsts of what Romana Bahry called the "fourth wave of rock music" in Ukraine, which began, in a bizarre coincidence, on the same evening as the explosion of the Chernobyl nuclear reactor on April 26, 1986. On that date, "the first independent rock music concert" was held at Kyiv University's faculty of foreign languages—although, since there was no live sound equipment available, the "concert" consisted solely of recordings played back in DAT or MiniDisc formats. *Fonohraf* co-organized another concert of rock music later that year, on October 29, now in collaboration with institutions that could provide live sound. The festival, called Debut '86, reportedly drew a crowd of 1,200 to a hall with the capacity for 800, and featured ten Kyiv-based bands who had "previously played only in cellars and apartments."[16] It was, quite literally, the public debut of the Kyiv underground.

In 1988, *Fonohraf* expanded its mandate again, and became the first enterprise to "release music on cassette tapes in the Ukrainian Soviet Socialist Republic, and later in Ukraine."[17] The idea to get into the tape replication business started with

---

[15]Richard Sakwa, *Gorbachev and His Reforms (1985–1990)*, 2nd ed. (New York: Prentice Hall, 1991), 292.

[16]Bahry, 246.

[17]This quote is taken from a 2018 interview for the online magazine *Amnesia* archived at: amnesia.in.ua/tapes.

the January 13, 1988 issue of *Fonohraf*, where the editors had invited nominations for the top nine songs that readers wanted to hear. Nominations poured in, along with requests as to where recordings of this music could be obtained. But, recordings of the Kyivan underground did not exist in an official sense; besides the person-to-exchange of so-called *magnitizdat*, there was nowhere to go. An idea arose when Rudiachenko met Iakov Shkol'nyk, the director of the "creative workshop Fonohramma" later in January 1988 and an avid reader of *Fonohraf*. "Fonohramma" (Phonogram), based in the Central Park of Culture and Recreation of Kyiv, offered tape replication at a mass scale for state institutions such as folk groups, Pioneer ensembles, and the like. Shkol'nyk offered to help replicate tapes for the *Fonohraf* readership too, starting with a collection of the top ten songs from the annual hit parade, which would be culled together from *magnitizdat* recordings.

Fonohraf journalists proposed this idea to the readership in the next issue, printing an interview with Shkol'nyk that included the question: "So if we understand correctly, "Fonohramma" offers *Fonohraf* their cooperation"?

The response from readers assured them that there would be massive consumer demand. Ultimately, however, Fonohramma could not assist in replicating the tapes because they were overwhelmed with their more official work. So, the journalists of *Fonohraf* decided to forge their own cooperative, which they would also call *Fonohraf*. Much of that year was spent doing the administrative work necessary to establish the new cooperative, work that they were "figuring out from zero." No one had experience in commerce, accounting, or relevant skills, but eventually, an individual named Serhiy Zhdanov, who had been working in video commerce (one of the early

Є пропозиція!

«ФОНОГРАМА» КАЖЕ: «А...»

Попередній випуск «Фонографа» [див. «МГ» від 13.I. ц. р.] був повністю присвячений підсумкам минулого року, що підбивалися за дев'ятьма категоріями. Це викликало чималу пошту. Лунали й телефонні дзвінки. Одни із них зацікавив своєю оперативністю та конкретною пропозицією, а головне, прагненням надати практичну допомогу культпрацівникам (особливо з сільської місцевості, районів області), які, до речі, часто пишуть нам про численні проблеми, пов'язані з організацією та проведенням дискотек, вечорів відпочинку для молоді тощо. Отже, наш співрозмовник — завідуючий творчою майстернею «Фонограм» Центрального парку культури і відпочинку Києва Яків ШКОЛЬНИК:

— Виявляється, ми вже сьогодні готові зробити добірку фонограм за музичною анкетою «Молодої гвардії».
— Дуже цікаво. Що ви маєте на увазі?
По перше, втім, що ми вашу газету передплачуємо, а випуски «Фонографа», загалі, уважно вивчаємо: хочеться знати, що саме і чому сьогодні слухає чи прагне слухати молодь Києва. По-друге, — і це вже конкретна пропозиція: наша творча майстерня регулярно готує нові

добірки розважальної музики. Тож і подумалося: а чому б не зробити добірку «Десять кращих пісень року з точки зору читачів «Фонографа». Думаю, дехто захоче мати їх і у фонотеці, на шкільній дискотеці і таке інше.
— А які ваші умови?
— Якщо когось детальніше зацікавить наша робота, можемо надіслати конкретні проспекти з пропозиціями творчої майстерні. Але «Фонограм» виконує замовлення шкіл, організацій, підприємств і установ тільки за безготівковим розрахунком. Листи з конкретними пропозиціями можете надсилати або в «Молоду гвардію» (з поміткою «Фонограф»), або безпосередньо нам: Київ-1, Володимирський узвіз, 2, Центральний парк культури і відпочинку, «Фонограма».
— Як ми зрозуміли, «Фонограма» пропонує «Фонографу» співробітництво?
— Так. І хочемо запевнити всіх читачів вашої газети, що листи з конкретними пропозиціями (якщо такі будуть, звичайно) ми обов'язково візьмемо до уваги, випускаючи черговий звуковий «хіт-парад» «Молодої гвардії».
— Спасибі. Отже, ВАША ДУМКА: культорганізатори, диск-жокеї, меломани. Вам — не лише пропозиція, але й гарантована послуга.

ФОНОГРАММА

252001, КИЕВ, ВЛАДИМИРСКИЙ СПУСК 2. ЦПКиО. ТВОРЧЕСКАЯ МАСТЕРСКАЯ «ФОНОГРАММА» тел 229-50-79

ОРИГИНАЛ ФОНОГРАММЫ

• СКОРОСТЬ
• КОЛ-ВО ДОРОЖЕК
• ВРЕМЯ ЗВУЧАНИЯ
• ЗАКАЗ №
• ДАТА
• ОПЕРАТОР
• РЕДАКТОР

Figure 2.5 *The Fonohraf article proposing a cassette-purchasing scheme. From the personal archives of O. Rudiachenko. Used with permission.*

Tusovka

lucrative cooperative businesses), joined their team. Through acquaintances they found a location in the House of Youth (Будинок Побуту "Молодіжний"), where they could rent two or three rooms on the first floor. The address was vul. Artema 15 (renamed to Sichovykh Striltsiv after 1991). They outfitted the space for tape-dubbing, where they would make copies of existing *magnitoalbomy* of the Russian rock scene. Eventually, they started hosting film screenings of foreign musical films such as *Jesus Christ Superstar* and *Hair*. Within six months, however, Rudiachenko told me that "the paradigm changed again" and they realized that, rather than replicating these Russian bootlegs, they could focus on their Kyivan *tusovka*, making cost-effective copies of domestic music that did not get exposure on radio or television. Since access to printers was highly controlled at the time, they came up with the ingenious idea to print the cover art for their cassette releases in the newspaper, marked off by scissors and a dotted line. Readers would bring this cover art to their space, and "the operator would know what to do"[18] (see Figure 1.3).

Rudiachenko, with advice from Yevtushenko, decided that VV's *Tantsi* should be the first release, because the band had consistently appeared in the top five of the *Fonohraf* hit parade. In a 2018 interview for the online magazine *Amnesia* (amnesia. in.ua), Rudiachenko offered some additional details on *Fonohraf*'s tape releasing activities:

> The first album of the studio was *Tantsi* by the group VV, which appeared on March 29, 1989. The circulation, I think, did not exceed 200 items. Having seen the insert in *MG,* you could travel to 15 vul. Artema and order a cassette for yourself.

---

[18]Personal interview, January 5, 2022.

We released mainly Ukrainian bands, very rarely Russian ones. For the price at the time, cassettes were affordable, though I don't remember for sure. The first three years of the existence of *Fonohraf* could be called educational. Money was not generated through such activities. The next two years— *monkey business* [original in English]. Those who wanted to make money opened a video salon. Without digging up the archives, I would estimate that 150 to 200 albums were released in the history of the studio.

After releasing the cassette of *Tantsi*, Yevtushenko then reviewed the album in the next issue of *Fonohraf*, writing that there are "fourteen tracks of varying caliber, alchemized of petulant Ukrainian folk-punk. Listening to it, you will have many thoughts. Except one: what is all this? From a pretty beaten-up banner, on which is written 'ТАНЦІ'—the biggest hit in Ukraine—the quartet with the original bayan and saxophone-playing Oleg Skrypka invents post-industrial dance parties. In comparison with them the [Stalinist psychiatric] clinic of Pavlov would appear to be a sanatorium for the mentally healthy."[19]

By linking the newspaper to the concert organizing enterprise to the cassette dubbing collective, Rudiachenko made *Fonohraf* into a circular economy shielded, through its association with the official Komsomol newspaper, from extensive meddling from censors and bureaucrats. From the protected hub of *Fonohraf*, the spokes of culture on the edge of officialdom connected to fully underground enterprises

---

[19]My translation from the original Ukrainian in Yevtushenko's *Fonohraf* review in 1989.

such as the numerous *samizdat* publications that circulated information about musicians and fans.

Huchnomovets; or, Loudspeaker

> Before you, dear reader, is the first issue of the Kyivan journal *Huchnomovets*. This is the brainchild of a small group of people in love with rock music. In Kyiv there have been, and continue to be, similar publications, like "Kimik," and "Subjecticon," but really these are very thin. And their circulation is also small. The editors of *Huchnomovets* have more promising plans: we want people to know about Kyivan rock music not only locally, but in other cities too.

With this opening salvo from the editor, the inaugural issue of the *samizdat* journal *Huchnomovets* declared its ambitions in April 1988. *Huchnomovets* positioned itself as the brash new loudspeaker for "the most interesting Kyivan groups." The typewritten opening editorial page continues: "Attention! Attention!! Attention!! The new Kyiv rock publication *Huchnomovets* speaks, reflects, gossips, doubts, laughs"![20] At the bottom of the page, the editors include alternative names for the enterprise—including the Russian name "matiugalnyk,"

---

[20]A 2015 live journal entry names additional small-scale Kyivan samizdat publications including *Bonba* (Бонба; two issues in 1988); *Zhopa* (Жопа; three issues between Feb 1990 and March 1991); *Manifest* (Манифест; one issue in 1989); *Subjecticon* (Субъектикон; five issues between 1987 and 1989); *Panok* (Панок; eight issues between 1988 and 1989); and КиМіик (Kimik, short for "Kyivan microphone"). https://starovina.livejournal.com/305705.html, accessed May 7, 2021. The first known interview with VV appeared in *Subjecticon* in early 1988.

Figure 2.6 *The cover of the inaugural issue of* Huchnomovets, *April 1988. The cover was designed by Konstantyn Kravchenko based on a photo by Oleksiy Zaika. From the personal archives of T. Yezhova. Used with permission.*

meaning "a device that swears"—again asserting itself as an unrepentant mouthpiece for the youth of the Kyivan musical *tusovka*.

Edited by the sibling duo of Tatyana and Nikolai Yezhov, *Huchnomovets* lived up to its promise to popularize Kyivan rock music beyond the city. In fact, it shored up connections between other prominent rock hubs, especially the Leningrad rock scene whose magazine *Roxy* had inspired the Yezhova siblings to create the Kyivan journal. Published in six issues between 1988 and 1990, *Huchnomovets* (according to the journalist Sherman Drozd) "became a real monument to the collapse of the USSR." Printed on a typewriter through a carbon copy, the pages were then supplemented with pasted-in photographs before some numbers of copies (usually about twenty in total) were circulated freely to leaders of the local rock scene.

As it became more established, *Huchnomovets* featured articles by a geographically dispersed array of individuals, some of whom would later go on to prominence in the fields of literature, art, and music. These included a then-teenaged Eugene Hütz, who authored articles under the name Evgeny Nikolaev, and would later go on to global fame as the dynamic front man of the punk-cabaret band Gogol Bordello. Volodymyr Nesterenko (now a writer and screenwriter with a cult following) published under the name "Adol'fych," the impresario Oleg "Mokh" Gnativ (famous for his association with Hutsul-punk band Perkalaba), and the Tallinn rock journalist Nikolai Meinert all contributed writing. *Huchnomovets*, then, did not merely amplify—it operated also as a megaphone for a variety of characters who would not otherwise have had a public voice to champion the bands they adored.

VV were heroes for *Huchnomovets*, appearing in every issue of the *samizdat* publication, often featured in multiple essays that ranged from scene reports to critical appraisals. Their impact on the Ukrainian rock scene was taken up in the first issue, April 1988, by an author who signed only with the initials NES (НЭС).[21] (This article followed another one also dedicated to the subject of VV.) Sardonic, teeming with linguistic jokes and Russian slang—the dominant language in Kyiv at the time, and the dominant language of the Kyivan youth scene—the author, writing in the wake of the 1986 Chernobyl nuclear disaster, opines on VV's songs as exemplifying "the music of the outskirts":

> Tension appears at the edges, heated by the pulpy beams of the center, under the heat of which paneled high-rise buildings rise like mushrooms. The center has become dead, clogged with the gray granite of government agencies … With the appearance of VV arose "Ukrainian rock"—bizarre music, strange voices. The desire to speak out—for too long a time Kyiv was sheared under the same blond comb as the capital and Piter.[22] Although with the "national" particularities, of course, we always had everything in order—our overripe mother WELCOMED GOOD PEOPLE, FLOWERING RUE-MINT, drowning out the strumming of guitars in the twilight of the city outskirts.[23] To understand that here was another zone, you needed a good kick. Today's Ukraine—a Ukraine of solid brick "private traders," clogging the grocery stores with products, Ukraine in the "epoch of prosperity"—has approached the line beyond which is the unknown; in front

---

[21] According to Tatyana Yezhova, this was the *nom de plume* of Oleg Berenstein.
[22] St. Petersburg, or—at the time this was written, Leningrad.
[23] This phrase mocks the folklorizing rhetoric that Soviet ideologists used to describe Ukraine, and places it as the inferior, less modern, younger sibling to the Russian big brother.

of which is confusion, reflected in the "Wails … " ["Vopli"] of the *veveshnyky*.[24]

Local castles in the sky are contaminated with radiation. Restricted area …

The "Ukrainian punk" of VV … stands closer to Ukrainian *kolomyiky-koliada*[25] than to classic rock, the child of sultry Africa, the big cosmopolitan. Is this a new direction?

Or a new dead end?[26]

Although the author lands here on an ambiguous and somewhat menacing question, VV's significance in the scene—especially as the originators of Ukrainophone "Ukrainian rock"— is beyond question. What strikes me is that, even in the seemingly ambivalent analysis of the author, VV is interpreted as having reconfigured Kyiv's place on the map of the USSR, especially in its relationship to Moscow and Leningrad. In this sense, VV places the Kyivan *tusovka* on the cultural map as a new center, not as a derivative periphery.

Despite its short life and extremely limited circulation, *Huchnomovets* became an important chronicler of the factions that came to define the Kyiv rock scene as it effectively split between the metalheads, and the punk and alternative bands.

---

[24]*Veveshnyky* is the term used to describe the members of the band VV. This last phrase can be read as the "Vopli of the Veveshnyky."

[25]This phrase refers to two iconic Ukrainian musical forms: the *kolomyika* sung poems associated with Western Ukraine, and the traditional caroling practices of *koliada*.

[26]This is my translation from the original (mostly) Russian text. Terms in caps appear in caps in the original; they are also the only Ukrainian-language words in the essay. Enormous thanks to Tatyana Yezhova, the editor of *Huchnomovets*, who scanned the first three issues for me, and mailed me a physical copy of writing from *Huchnomovets* that was re-published in 1993. This excerpt from issue no. 1 appears on page 16 in this collection.

The publication unequivocally cast its lot with the trio of bands—Kollezhskyi Asessor, VV, and Vavylon, who renamed themselves Rabbota XO in April 1988—who eventually left the official infrastructure of the Kyiv Rock Club as it grew inhospitable to groups whose aesthetic approaches did not comport with the mainstream heavy metal culture privileged there. These three bands, under the leadership of Volodymyr Ivanov, their entrepreneurial manager at the time, broke off to form a new "experimental" union known as Rock Artil.

The Kyiv Rock Club and the Experiment

The famous Kyiv Rock Club "Kuznia," following long-term conciliatory Komsomol meetings and a great "war of nerves," was, finally, opened in 1986 at the House of Culture "Bilshovyk." The rockers received a concert hall and a few rehearsal spaces. And everyone was very happy. And no one objected to the fact that the Komsomol-curator would control everything—the texts of the songs, the participation or non-participation of groups in the Club's events.

Oleksandr Yevtushenko, *Ukraïna IN ROCK*

Located in the basement of 38 Prospect Peremohy in the Palace of Culture "Bilshovyk," across the street from the Kyiv Polytechnic Institute, the Kyiv Rock Club (Рок-Клуб) was established in the fall of 1986. Known colloquially as the "Kuznia" (Кузня, meaning "The Forge"), the elder statesman of Ukrainian rock, Kyrylo Stetsenko, who came to the Kuznia to scout up-and-coming talents for his television program, compared the dank basement venue to the kind of "place where the NKVD tortured people in the 1930s."[27]

Inspired by similar entities that had formed under the auspices of the Komsomol in other cities—such as the influential Leningrad Rock Club (founded in 1981)—the Kyiv Rock Club came together when two hard rock bands, Edem and Kvartyra 50, appealed to local authorities for an official location and funding support for the bands who would become founding club members. Volodymyr Ivanov, who served on the artistic council (художня рада) of the Kyiv Rock Club for a time, recalled how the Komsomol operated as both the protective "shelter and the censor" for the Kyivan rock *tusovka*.[28] He added, however, that having a sanctioned venue—even if it was a basement in the House of Culture—was transformational for him and other music fans. Ivanov reminisced about the visceral and psychological impact of hearing live loud rock music for the first time, not just scratchy bootlegs or pirated vinyl—how it sated the hunger that he and other fans had, how the sound coursed through his body and made him want to hear more.

Despite being the first official place to hear live rock music, the "Kuznia" was short-lived. In the 1989 *Fonohraf Digest*, the former president of the Kyiv Rock Club Yuri Sakhno (no relation to VV's drummer) wrote about conflicts over material conditions as well as aesthetic principles. Romana Bahry explained that because of "many managerial and administrative problems such as the lack of a distinction between professional and amateur groups, lack of material support from sponsors, and commercial and marketing problems, the association

---

[27]Personal interview, January 2, 2022.
[28]Personal interview, January 3, 2022.

came to an end."[29] Still, during its less-then-two-year window of existence, the Kyiv Rock Club became an essential infrastructure through which bands could seek some form of legitimacy and state support. Registering with local authorities as "amateur (самодіяльні) bands" afforded them access to rehearsal spaces, prizes, and billing on official concerts. Becoming legitimate in the eyes of the authorities could require, depending on the moment in *perestroika* reforms, processes of vetting and censorship called *litovannia* and *taryfikatsia*; procedures I will explore in detail in Chapter four of this book.

VV entered the Kyiv Rock Club in the fall of 1987, generating what Tatyana Yezhova, the editor of *Huchnomovets* and devotee of the Kyivan scene, described as a "scandal."[30] The band, having just gained membership to the Rock Club thanks to the machinations of their entrepreneurial new manager Volodya Ivanov, took first place in the Rock Parade (Рок-Парад) festival organized to celebrate the Rock Club's first anniversary. They won in the categories of "Band of the Year" and "Best Song of the Year" with the song "Yaroslavna's Lament" (Plach Yaroslavny, or Плач Ярославни).[31] Yezhova recounted the scandal in full in her LiveJournal blog on November 15, 2011,

---

[29]Bahry 1994, 246.

[30]Personal interview, December 5, 2021.

[31]The title of this song will be familiar to students of Ukrainian and Russian history. "Yaroslavna's Lament" is the title of a famous poem by the romantic poet-hero of Ukraine, Taras Shevchenko. Shevchenko's poem, in turn, is based upon a fragment from the medieval Old East Slavic epic poem known in English as "The Tale of Igor's Campaign." In the epic poem, Yaroslavna is Igor's wife. Worried about her husband's fate during an ill-fated military campaign against the invading Polovtsians, she calls upon natural forces (sun, wind, and water) to confirm his loss. Much of the action of the poem takes place on the territory of modern-day Ukraine. Finally, in Alexander Borodin's late-nineteenth-century opera *Prince Igor*, "Yaroslavna's Lament" is a centerpiece.

reminiscing about a concert that had occurred twenty-four years earlier to the day:

> What can I remember? It was great. November is damp and already quite cold. Getting to the Sovremennik Hall in Frunze Park required multiple transfers. The equipment, to put it mildly, was not at the level of world standards and so you can imagine the quality of sound … But—the crowd in front of the entrance, the excitement in the hall and the sea of buzz, pure buzz! Maybe this was because everyone was young, energetic, and rock and roll in Kyiv was still a novelty. I am thinking now: who would lure me to a concert like this on such a cold evening now, on November 15, 2011?

Given their new status as members of the Rock Club, VV's victories were not received well by many of the Kyiv Rock Club founders. Kyrylo Stetsenko wrote that the anniversary concert "marked how the balance of power in Kyiv rock showed a decline of interest in metal."[32] The resentments this engendered deepened to the point that VV (along with Kollezhskyi Asessor and Rabbota XO) broke from the Rock Club and formed a new cooperative in December 1987. Their manager, Volodymyr Ivanov, proposed the name for their union (Rock Artil), forging it under the umbrella of an existing association called "Experiment" (Товариство "Експеримент"). In February 1988, Rock Artil sponsored their first rock concert in the dance hall at Kyiv's Holosiivsky Park.

According to Oleksandr Yevtushenko, "Rock Artil was a kind of antipode to the metal-hard rock *tusovka* of the Rock Club

LitMir Electronic Library, (https://lehautparleur.livejournal.com/150852.html, accessed December 9, 2021.).

Kuznia."[33] It quickly gained a cultish following and international success—the trio of bands started touring to other Soviet states almost immediately, starting with the Tallinn Rock Festival in early 1988, concerts in Moscow, and later Poland and France. Rock Artil was evidence of the ways in which "the rock club was partially strangled by the cooperative movement," in the words of the Russian music journalist Alexander Kushnir, who pointed to the "chic Rock Artil of Kyiv" as evidence of this in a 2021 interview.[34]

Much of Rock Artil's success had to do with the gumption of Volodymyr Ivanov, a gregarious sculptor and rock music fan who became well-connected in the Kyivan rock *tusovka* because of his involvement in the 1987 "Youth of the Country" (Молодість Країни) art exhibition. Responsible for the cultural program of the youth-oriented exhibition, he helped organize the "Rock Dialogue" festival, which then led to invitations to join the artistic board of the newly created Kyiv Rock Club. In April 1987, following the open-air performance of amateur rock groups for Kyiv Day, he met Yuri Zdorenko and Sashko Pipa, who gave him a demo cassette of VV's songs. A few weeks later, he visited them during a rehearsal, where—he told me—he was perhaps "the first person to hear the newly born hit 'Tantsi.'" In October of that year, Ivanov organized the first public performance for VV, who played between film screenings at the Kyiv Film Festival "Molodist." And in November 1987, he argued for their late inclusion in the Rock Club's anniversary competition, where they triumphed over the more established metal bands of the scene, as described in Yezhova's testimony above.

---

[33]Yevtushenko, *Ukraïna IN ROCK*.
[34]The interview with Kushnir was on TACC.RU, https://tass.ru/kultura/10836803, accessed January 2022

At some point in 1987, Ivanov became VV's "manager," though the notion hardly existed at the time.[35] Ivanov created their merch—buttons and banners with the slogans "Tantsi" and "Long Live VV" (Хай Живе ВВ)—an irreverent twist on the formulaic Soviet slogans that championed Lenin's eternal life, socialist revolution, or other ideologically appropriate people and events. It was Ivanov who brought VV's music to the influential rock critic Artemy Troitsky, which led to—among other things—their participation in a 1988 documentary film, made by French TV channel Antenne-2, titled "Rock Around the Kremlin." The documentary featured VV performing their song "Buly Den'ki" (There Were Days) on a square in Moscow, and fed their popularity in France, where Skrypka and Pipa lived intermittently after 1991.[36] Ivanov organized rehearsal spaces, festival appearances, and touring logistics for the band, and "settled conflictual situations between the Komsomol and concert organizers, as well as conflicts between groups." Ivanov explained to me that this was a volunteer position, "a hobby" to which he devoted considerable energy on top of his professional (and compensated) work as a sculptor. "I was involved with the group when it was not really a commercial enterprise; during concerts and tours in the best situations they

---

[35]Ivanov wrote to me to clarify that the term "manager" did not really exist. "For some reason, he said, we used the term 'director' back then."

[36]From 1991 to 1996, VV was based between France and Ukraine. After Zdorenko left the group in 1993, the two other members of the band were French musicians. In 1996, Pipa and Skrypka moved back to Kyiv, and the original drummer (Serhiy Sakhno) re-joined the group. They also invited their former teenaged fan, Yevhen Rohachevsky, to play guitar. At the time of writing, in 2022, Sakhno and Rohachevsky are still playing with VV though Rohachevsky has been serving in the Ukrainian Armed Forces since the Russian full-scale invasion.

would cover our costs."[37] It was not for the money back then, he indicated, but for the music and the fun. Though Ivanov and the bands of Rock Artil discontinued their work together in 1989 (before the *Fonohraf* release of *Tantsi*), his energetic advocacy for these Kyivan bands had a profound effect on the landscape of Soviet youth musical subcultures domestically and abroad.

A series of comics featured in the fifth issue of *Huchnomovets* (published in 1989) retells the story of the creation of the Rock Artil. In six panels (reproduced below), the viewer learns the history of VV:

Figure 2.7 *Comic created by Volodymyr Mulyk for the fifth issue of* Huchnomovets, *1989. From the personal archives of T. Yezhova. Used with permission by T. Yezhova and V. Mulyk.*

[37]Personal interview, January 4, 2022.

1) Pipa and Zodrenko play metal in SOS,

2) Pipa introduces Skrypka to Zdorenko, saying "he is going to play with us"! and abandoning the aesthetics of heavy metal in 1987

3) Spring of 1987, at the Rock Club in front of a panel of censors who tell them, "No! We do not need this music here"!

4) Nov 1987, their manager Volodya Ivanov asks for them to be included in the Rock Parade festival at the Rock Club,

5) the overwhelming vote for VV following their performance at the Rock Parade, and finally

6) the band being cast out of the Rock Club for being "demagogues" and moving to an open door labeled "Experiment."

Similar pages exist for the other two bands who left the Rock Club for Rock Artil, each culminating in their expulsion from the Rock Club and opening the door to "Experiment." The fourth page of the comic illustrates how the bands of Rock Artil were able to tour to Vladivostok, Moscow, Warsaw, and Vilnius; until, in 1989, VV left Rock Artil in pursuit of new opportunities.

Balka: Black-market Music

Every narrative of the Kyiv rock scene seems to begin with Balka, the black-market bazaar where *melomany* would gather to meet, purchase vinyl illegally imported from the West, trade cassettes, and share knowledge about the unofficial music scene. Balka is where Oleksandr Yevtushenko first met Oleksandr Rudiachenko, which led to Yevtushenko joining the writing team for *Fonohraf* in early 1987. Balka was where Nikolai Yezhov, Tatyana's older brother, learned about the music that inspired the siblings to start *Huchnomovets*. Balka was where the *neformaly* of Kyiv found each other. It was where young people pooled their resources to buy expensive vinyl, held on to it long enough to dub it to cassette, and then sold it back. From the mid-1970s, when record collectors with bags of illicit records converged in various meetings places around Kyiv—near the botanical garden, in a ravine amid railroad tracks, by the cycling track near the circus, at the Sovremennik Hall—Balka was where friendships started, bands were formed, and alliances solidified. VV's first manager Volodymyr Ivanov—who also patronized Balka in the 1980s—told me that "everyone who went there either became a musician or a fan."

Balka was the place where VV bassist Sashko Pipa spotted his English teacher. This teacher had only recently started teaching at the Kyiv Polytechnic University, where Pipa and the other members of VV were students. At the first lesson, he taught them to pronounce the words "Deep Purple," cuing them to his subcultural leanings. When, at Balka, he saw his teacher run from the police breaking up the black market (as they did nearly every week), his suspicions were confirmed: his teacher was cool. When I asked if this was scary at all, if it weighed on his conscience or undermined the teacher's authority, Pipa responded by explaining that "there was a lot of illegal stuff that everyone did." This confirms an observation made by Thomas Cushman of the Leningrad rock musicians, who "went on with little conscious thought about whether or not such acts would be considered politically deviant."[38] Balka,

---

[38]Personal interview October 11, 2021; Thomas Cushman, *Notes from Underground: Rock Music Counterculture in Russia* (Albany: State University of New York Press, 1995), 93–4.

therefore, was precisely the kind of ad hoc infrastructure that allowed these youth scenes to operate in oblique relationships to state power.

A 2014 LiveJournal post by a user identified only as "flackelf" presented black and white photos of Kyiv in 1984 and included details on the Balka bazaar, which convened at that time at the Kyiv botanical garden, off of the "University" stop on the Metro. This person had just finished his second year at a technical school, which delayed his army service for up to two years. He had recently acquired a stereo cassette recorder (a "Mayak-232"), which he described as a "miracle of technology that cost as much as 355 rubles." Cassettes, he reported, were also expensive—a "whopping nine rubles," which amounted to eighteen meals in the technical school cafeteria or 180 trips on the Metro. A classmate brought him to what he described as "the so-called Balka: the illegal gangway between the buyers and sellers of imported discs." There, he acquired an Iron Maiden record from 1983.[39] "flackelf" described his sheer delight at the acquisition—until he realized he had been sold an Italian knockoff, and therefore had been overcharged according to Balka's black-market logics. "It would be several months until I learned how to stay in the positive at 'Balka.'"[40]

Balka appears here last on my list of essential ad hoc infrastructures of the Kyiv rock scene, but that should not be read as minimizing its importance. Based on the testimonies of the many individuals I interviewed, it was the source of many

[39]In 1985, Iron Maiden would appear on a list of "groups and artists whose repertoires contain ideologically harmful compositions" and were therefore banned from Soviet discotheques. Iron Maiden was indicted on the list for their "violence and religious obscurantism" (Yurchak 2005, 215).

[40]See https://flackelf.livejournal.com/414603.html, accessed December 3, 2021.

of the activities that would define the Kyivan underground. Sashko Pipa called it first, a site of "education"; second, a site of "connection."[41] Balka connected individuals to the official, semi-official, and unofficial publications; to the underground and Komsomol-operated venues. It was a central node in an interdependent scene. By convening the segment of Kyivans who refused the constraints of censorship and control that existed over musical cultures in the late Soviet period, Balka and these other ad hoc infrastructures formed the platform from which musicians, writers, and fans could identify their musical scenes.

Scene Report

In an October 2021 interview for the Ukrainian magazine *Telegid*, Oleg Skrypka was asked how he remembered the late 1980s in Kyiv. He answered that they were "turbulent times. Everything was changing, everywhere there were lots of ideas about new rock music. Then there were the *tusovki* that formed around cafes in the center: that's where progressive young people talked about music or gathered in apartments to listen to vinyl or sing together. Among our friends were erudite-encyclopedists, who knew a lot of interesting things about music and who opened the eyes of us, the rockers."[42] Similarly, in "Crank the Sound, Please!" (Дайте Звук, Будь Ласка!), the two-part documentary produced by the veterans of *Huchnomovets*, many key figures from the late 1980s Kyiv

---

[41]Personal interview, October 11, 2021.
[42]My translation from the Ukrainian: telegid.com/2021/10/13/олег-скрипка-вв-вибух-музичної-ес/.

musical *tusovka* are asked to reflect upon and characterize the scene that they had taken part in some thirty years earlier. One person responds that it was "fueled by coffee and beer" (back when beer cost only fifty-two kopeks). Another says that its special quality was in its diversity (різноманітність) and embrace of experiment. Another reminisces about all the time drinking coffee and hanging out at places such as Café Dontesk, languid hours full of conversation about art and music, casual plotting on how to work, skirt, or mock the system. From the cafés to the apartments to the Rock Club to the festival stages, the *tusovka* net widened out, networking together the *neformaly* of Kyiv and emboldening them to create.

When considering the entirety of Kyiv's underground *tusovka*—the one overlayed onto the map of the Kyivan Metro crafted so meticulously by the late Oleksandr Yevtushenko in that 1991 issue of *Fonohraf*—it is this cross-pollination of sites and people that nourished the richly hybrid experiments of VV, who, despite being relative latecomers to the scene, emerged swiftly as one of Kyiv's most iconic bands. Consider the journalists, the metalheads, the *Komosmoltsi*, the avant-gardists, the indie acts, the theatrical post-punks, the sculptors, the black-market vinyl traders, *samizdat* publishers, poets, and the dissidents of an older generation who crossed paths in the various ad hoc infrastructures of the scene. Across these spaces, they created something new from below amid rapid change from above. With no roadmap and considerable barriers, this *tusovka* nonetheless set a foundation for a future of Ukrainian music. *Tantsi*, with its funny absurdity and often-ambiguous parody, is one time capsule from this place, an artifact that only survives today because of the various ad hoc infrastructures that supported its coming into being.

3   Total *Stiob*: Irony vs. Hypocrisy

– Tell me, was the work of VV originally stiob, or not entirely?
– Of course it was stiob. In general, as soon as I took a guitar into my hands, I decided that one should not take music too seriously, especially rock.

Yuri Zdorenko[1]

In his 2011 book chronicling Ukrainian popular music, the journalist Oleksandr Yevtushenko rhapsodized about the ways in which VV "transformed street slang and rudeness into an aesthetics of total *stiob*."[2] *Stiob* is a slang term used in Ukrainian and Russian to describe a mode of late Soviet irony.[3] The anthropologist Alexei Yurchak defines it this way: "*Stiob* was a peculiar form of irony that differed from sarcasm, cynicism, derision, or any of the more familiar genres of absurd humor. It required such a degree of *overidentification* with the object, person, or idea at which this *stiob* was directed that it was

---

[1] 2012 interview with Aleskey Gusak, accessed at https://aleksey-gusak. livejournal.com/31107.html, January 18, 2022. My translation from the Russian.
[2] Yevtushenko, *Ukraïna IN ROCK*, 143. In the passage where Yevtushenko employs the phrase "total *stiob*" he compares VV's aesthetics to the *stiob*-ish characteristics of the L'viv-based rock band *Braty Hadiukiny* (Snake Brothers).
[3] Lesia Stavyts'ka, *Ukrainskiy Zharhon* (Kyiv: Krytyka, 2005). In her *Dictionary of Ukrainian Slang*, Stavyt'ska offers a few definitions of *stiob,* starting with a "mockingly aggressive, to some extent paradoxical way of thinking and orientation to the surrounding environment" (205).

often impossible to tell whether it was a form of sincere support, subtle ridicule, or a peculiar mixture of the two."[4] Such deadpan performances of *overidentification* spawn paradoxical effects: in refusing to reveal itself as parody, *stiob* so closely resembled ideologically "correct" forms that it eluded Soviet censorship regimes, while also sometimes appearing to reinforce the very structures it was parodying. *Stiob* also "did not occupy or promote recognizable political positions—it existed to some extent outside the familiar axes of political tensions between state and opposition, between Left and Right, aware of these axes but uninvested in them."[5]

In a 2010 article titled "American Stiob," Yurchak and Boyer gloss two famous *stiob* performances from the nonconformist Russian musician Sergei Kuryokhin: first, when he published an indictment of Soviet rockers in *Leningradskaya Pravda*, mimicking the condemnatory style of the "war on rock" so expertly that it confused both ideologues and rockers as to its sincerity: "it became evident to many readers that a text written in that language, and published in a central party newspaper, could be simultaneously an exemplary ideological statement and a public ridicule of that statement"[6] Second, they reviewed the most daredevil of Kuryokhin's feats of *stiob,* when—over the course of a ninety-minute television special aired on Soviet television in May 1991—he advanced a theory that Lenin habitually consumed so many hallucinogenic mushrooms

---

[4]Yurchak 2005, 250; for Yurchak's earliest publications on *stiob*, see "Gagarin and the Rave Kids: Transforming Power, Identity, and Aesthetics in the Post-Soviet Night Life," in *Consuming Russia: Popular Culture, Sex, and Society since Gorbachev,* ed. A. Baker (Durham: Duke University Press, 1999).

[5]Dominic Boyer and Alexei Yurchak, "American Stiob: Or, What Late-Socialist Aesthetics of Parody Reveal about Contemporary Political Culture in the West," *Cultural Anthropology* 25, no. 2 (2010): 182–3.

[6]ibid, 186.

that he had, in fact, "turned into a mushroom." Concluding his lecture, Kuryokhin stated: "I simply want to say that Lenin was a mushroom." It's ludicrous to read this summary now. But, as Yurchak argues, "what mattered was not simply *what* was presented but *how* it was presented": Kuryokhin's impersonation of a historian was so accurate, his delivery so stentorian, his jargon so scientific, that Soviet television audiences were forced to question the absurd thesis that Lenin could have been, in fact, a mushroom.[7] This is *stiob*, virtuosic *stiob*.

By refusing to align itself with clear political positions (either openly oppositional to or openly aligned with state power), *stiob* could provide an "ethical refuge" that allowed parodists to avoid fully "disenchant[ing] communist idealism," while exposing the hollowness of state-sanctioned forms of speech, comportment, and performance, and—as I will argue in this chapter—music. Yurchak and Boyer describe the "performative shift" that marked late Soviet discourse, when "it was often more meaningful to participate in the performative reproduction of the precise forms of authoritative discourse (as either producer or audience) than to concern oneself with what they might 'mean' in a literal sense."[8] Remember the

---

[7]"Kurekhin's [Kuryokhin's] audiences thought the claim appeared plausible, however, not because they were gullible enough to believe it, but because … Kurekhin had directed their attention away from the 'intrinsic quality' (literal meaning) of the statement and onto the flawlessness of the documents (provenance) supporting the statement." Alexei Yurchak, "A Parasite from Outer Space: How Sergei Kurekhin Proved That Lenin Was a Mushroom," *Slavic Review* 70, no. 2 (2011): 322. Yurchak and Boyer's 2010 article points to resonances in the parodic-ironic comedy of late liberalism in the US. They offer the example of *The Colbert Report*—in which the comedian Stephen Colbert *overidentified* with the bloviating former Fox News host Bill O'Reilly—as a paradigmatic example of "American Stiob" (189).
[8]Yurchak 2010, 182.

banners that so closely resembled the red and white *transpyranty* carried by the faithful Komsomol, with their perfectly blocky *Pravda* propaganda font? The banner that VV fans paraded onto stage when they sang "Tantsi"? The banner announced a simple, nonsensical slogan: DANCES. The visual form was overdetermined—legible so that any late Soviet citizen would recognize it as agitprop in a flash—but the politics are murky. What was VV agitating for exactly with that banner, beyond perhaps the obvious fact that they are dancing, and singing a song about dancing, and dancing is fun—especially when done in the riotous style of a Kyivan punk rocker? Can this be slotted into the seductive "resistance paradigm," with its "moralizing imperative" that marks so much anglophone writing on Soviet history, or does it instead confound the expected binary of resistance/acquiescence?[9]

In 2019, I asked Oleg Skrypka about *stiob* in VV's 1980s output. He answered by explaining that: "It all came very naturally, it wasn't a thought-out thing. There was an absolute rejection of the system (неприйняття системи) but also a clear understanding that protesting has no point, none." I'll note here that the average Ukrainian citizen of Skrypka's generation has had plenty of opportunity to reflect on questions about the efficacy of protest, given that his generation has lived through not only the rapid dissolution of the Soviet Union in 1991, but also two consequential post-Soviet revolutions in 2004 and 2013, and the ongoing brutal full-scale invasion of Ukraine by Russia in 2022 (though it is important to note that my interviews with him were conducted before February 24, 2022). In 2019, Skrypka ruminated on the efficacy of political protest in the Soviet and post-Soviet periods:

---

[9]Anna Krylova, "The Tenacious Liberal Subject in Soviet Studies," *Kritika: Explorations in Russian and Eurasian History* 1, no. 1 (2000), 139, 144.

And to this time I still think becoming occupied with revolution and going out on the street has no place; I'm convinced of this. And that's why you have to reject [the system] but do something else. Because when you are against something, directly, you remain within it … Instead, you just go to a different plane—this sarcasm *was* another plane. Only then can you build something new, really. But this is me philosophizing about it now. Back then it was clear that you couldn't accept what was; you just wanted to take part in what we thought of as pure art. But in principle, I don't think we really thought of anything that new because rock and roll was always fundamentally about protest, but also very cool, with so many different strains … it just happened twenty years later for us in the Soviet Union.

During this interview in 2019, I pushed back gently against the idea to which Skrypka arrived and asked whether he thought that the Soviet context of rock music framed the sarcasm, the humor, and irony in ways that were, perhaps, new. Skrypka conceded, to a point: "[our humor] was a kind of gallows humor, and the only person who can understand it is the one who sat in the prison; the person who didn't spend time in the prison can't grasp it."[10]

In defiance of Skrypka's warning, this chapter will nonetheless try to explain the joke: the humor that bristled against confinement, the ironic strategies of *overidentification* that shifted VV's *stiob* into total overdrive. If *stiob* can be understood as a kind of "weapon of the weak," VV perfected this weapon through intentionally oblique strategies that lampooned the untenable contradictions of late Soviet life, situating them

---

[10]Personal interview, June 5, 2019.

Total *Stiob*

specifically in a Soviet Ukrainian context.[11] My analysis of VV's *stiob* parallels elements of Yurchak and Boyer's analysis summarized above. Like them, I also draw on themes of linguistic *stiob* (VV's lyrics), and archetypal *stiob* (clothes, gestures, and stage imagery). But I also seek to extend the analysis in two ways. At the end of this chapter, I will consider *stiob* in relation to the aesthetics of musical sound, observing how practices of sonic imitation and excessive citation in VV's songs contributed to the effect of "total stiob" described by Yevtushenko. Importantly, this "total stiob" was not limited to lampooning the tensions of late Soviet life, but also mocked the preening self-serious masculinities of Western rock music culture. But first, I will bring the Soviet concept of *stiob* into dialogue with vernacular—especially rural—genres of Ukrainian irony. Sashko Pipa, the band's original bass player, was emphatic on the point that VV's *stiob* was heavily indebted to Ukrainian vernacular genres of humor: "in the Ukrainian village, everything is ironic."[12]

Pipa and I arrived at the topic of Ukrainian identity and language during an interview in May 2019, when I asked him about his personal linguistic choices: he is one of many Ukrainians who decided, after the 2014 Maidan Revolution, to convert fully to the Ukrainian language even though the Russian language had been his go-to in most contexts, as it had been for many Kyivans reared during the Soviet period. Pipa explained how, growing up, he thought of the Ukrainian language, basically, as uncool. As a teenager, however, he discovered the potentially subversive power of vernacular Ukrainian irony. Pipa explains it best:

---

[11] C. Scott, *Weapons of the Weak: Everyday Forms of Peasant Resistance* (New Haven: Yale University Press, 1985).
[12] Personal interview, May 13, 2019.

Because of the well-known history of Russian suppression of Ukrainian culture and the Russification of the Ukrainian language, more authentic Ukrainian language and traditions were preserved where Russification couldn't reach, so—in the village. I spent a lot of time as a child in the village in the Cherkassy region. And I became convinced that irony is just everywhere. When people talk, even about something serious, they are still constantly using some little catchphrases, some little half-jokes. Always. This is just a part of Ukrainian culture. The irony of irony itself. It's not in vain that Kotlarevsky's *Eneida* is an ironic translation of Virgil. And *Lys Mykyta* of Ivan Franko—also deeply ironic.[13]

And on the other hand—I am almost certain that the Communists did this deliberately—and I studied in a Ukrainian school, so the Ukrainian language was not banned. But in the classes on Ukrainian literature they forced us to read exclusively this dark, dark literature … a selection to associate Ukrainian language and culture with something boring, sad, something like that.

So, as a clear alternative, as a fight with oneself, there was irony. And I was a teenager in Russian-speaking Kyiv, in Russian-speaking Akademmistechko. If you spoke Ukrainian, it signified that you were an uneducated "redneck" [spoken in English] or a "Banderite."[14] On television there was a lot of

---

[13]Pipa refers here to two landmark works in the canon of Ukrainian literature. Ivan Kotlarevsky's parody of *The Aeneid* (published in pieces starting in 1798) is considered by many to mark the beginning of modern Ukrainian literature. It was suppressed in Imperial Russia because of its literary use of the Ukrainian language. Ivan Franko's famous poem *Lys Mykyta* (1902) is the other work referenced.

[14]"Banderite" refers to a WWII-nationalist leader, Stepan Bandera, who was (and remains in contemporary Russia) a kind of bogeyman figure. To be called a "Banderite" is to be called a Ukrainian nationalist, or fascist.

Ukrainian language, but it was always in this context—"the Ukrainian language is beautiful, it's the language of our bread-makers, and of the glorious past." But contemporary music, film comedies, documentation of outer space rockets—this was in Russian. It was the language of youth.

VV tried to break this consciousness. I once saw an interview with [the Ukrainian rock musician] Skryabin when he was in the army. He was Ukrainian speaking, from Western Ukraine, and while he was in the army he saw the video of "Tantsi" on the TV and only then thought to himself, well hell, you can even sing punk in Ukrainian. So, this idea hadn't occurred even to *him*—even though he was Ukrainian-speaking.

So, if there is a reason to build a statue to Skrypka for any reason, it should be for this. It was his accomplishment. Because he was raised in Russia, in Russian schools in Murmansk. And he knew Ukrainian very poorly. As a result, he didn't have these cliches, the Soviet imprint on his language. And that's why when he started writing texts, they were these bombs.

It was his [Skrypka's] idea. We weren't some idea-driven nationalists, this was just an artistic choice. Ukrainian really— it just sounds better in a song. And there were groups before us who had tried to sing in Ukrainian, but it sounded uninteresting. And this is where Skrypka's poetry played an important role.[15]

Pipa and the other members of VV, he told me, grew up in the "Russian world" (русский мир). They spoke Russian in their daily lives, at home, and with each other. For Pipa, Skrypka, and

[15]Personal interview, May 13, 2019.

many of the other individuals whom I interviewed between 2019 and early 2022 for this project, the awareness of themselves as Ukrainian, and the subsequent "fight with oneself" that Pipa names above, suggests strong resonances with the personal and political testimonies of canonical anti-colonial writers.

Much as in Memmi's tortured *The Colonizer and the Colonized,* many of the Ukrainians interviewed for this book had spent years trying to make sense of the "incoherent and contradictory" conditions of a colonized mentality. Memmi poses the question, "How could [the colonized] hate the colonizers and yet admire them so passionately"? He then implicates himself, in parentheses: "(I too felt this admiration in spite of myself.)"[16] Making sense of having been colonized is disorienting, and it is personal. Although it is beyond the scope here to review the vast literature debating whether or not Ukraine's relationship to the Soviet Union should be understood as a colonial relationship, what comes through in so many of my interviews is how many Ukrainians raised in the Soviet Union understand themselves now, in the twenty-first century, to be formerly colonized subjects.[17] This suggests one of the ugly time-scales of colonialism: it may take considerable time to recognize one's internalized sense of inferiority as a symptom

[16]Albert Memmi, *The Colonizer and the Colonized* (London: Earthscan Publications Ltd, 2003 [1957]), 6. Memmi's 1965 preface is critical of dogmatic either/or Marxist and psychoanalytic approaches to the study of colonization, rejecting that "all experience, all feeling, all suffering, all the byways of human behavior" could be reduced to either "profit motive or Oedipus complex" (9).
[17]I suspect that, after the full-scale brutal invasion of Ukraine in late February 2022, which many understand to be Putin's revanchist project to restore a pre-Soviet empire, this sense of having formerly been colonized has hardened among many demographics of Ukrainian citizens, while the Russian state continues to make the patently false claim that it was ever an empire.

Total *Striob*

73

of having been colonized. Kyrylo Stetsenko told me that, to him, the matter of identifying as Ukrainian was "anti-political; it was existential." Stetsenko recognized the Ukrainian "inferiority complex" (комплекс неповноцінності) as endemic to post-WWII Soviet Ukrainian society, as the pressure to conform to Russified modes of speech, comportment, and cultural expression were ubiquitous, promising individuals many material benefits in addition to precious forms of symbolic capital.[18]

The Ukrainian dissident Ivan Dziuba attested to the slow pace at which he arrived at the realization that he had been lying to himself about the neutrality of the Soviet cultural policies that seemed to breed malice towards Ukrainian culture:

> In my early student years, I was one of the countless people who "didn't care" what language they spoke and what nation they belonged to, and who were proud of their "indifference" as a standard of internationalism and universal values. And then I began to think: if it really does not matter, why are all those in Ukraine who are supposedly indifferent, not really indifferent (and sometimes hostile, consciously or unconsciously) only to the Ukrainian language, Ukrainian culture, and Ukraine in general? And where does their "indifference" and "international" impartiality vanish when it comes to the prestige of their acquired "Russianness"? Who and why do whole nations cease to be themselves and not create something new, but simply merge into another nation, depriving it of its own face? Is this the path to equality and universal solidarity?

---

[18]Personal interview, January 2, 2022.

For writing such observations at a moment of Soviet repression of the Ukrainian language, Dziuba was imprisoned in Siberia. Eventually, Dziuba was rehabilitated in the 1980s, and went on in his post-Soviet writings to suggest that the timescale of *unlearning* a postcolonial inferiority complex poses yet another set of bedeviling problems.[19]

And so, keeping in mind the chorus of voices attesting to their post-Soviet understanding of having been formerly colonized, it is critical to place the testimonies that I have gathered into their proper context: after all, more than three decades have elapsed since the social world that supported *Tuntsi* existed. To add, post-socialist memory politics are perhaps especially unstable—the Ukrainian "memory wars" of the post-Maidan period capture much of this complexity, and the Russian war on Ukraine further inflames the question of who has the right to claim memories of the past as a national patrimony.[20] My interviewees were acutely aware of the time and place that they were summoning in their memories, often remarking upon how their politics had sharpened into anti-colonial critique only after access to information became more freely available after the fall of the USSR. That is, only *after* they learned the history of Soviet repression of the Ukrainian language and the deliberate folklorization of its culture, only *after* they read Memmi (or Freire, Fanon, Ngũgĩ, and Césaire), only *after* they got access to the repressed poems of Vasyl Stus

---

[19]This passage appeared translated into English in this article: https://euromaidanpress.com/2022/02/23/in-memoriam-donbas-dissident-dziuba-jailed-by-ussr-for-challenging-russian-imperialism/, accessed February 24, 2022.
[20]Andrii Portnov, "Memory Wars in Post-Soviet Ukraine (1991–2010)," in *Memory and Theory in Eastern Europe*, ed. Uilleam Blacker, Alexander Etkind, and Julie Fedor (New York Palgrave Macmillan, 2013).

or any number of other late Soviet Ukrainian dissident writers, artists, and intellectuals.

For VV, the late 1980s pivot towards Ukrainian language marked a slow-moving shift in national consciousness that was accompanied by a great deal of awkwardness, and a disavowal of the politics of nationalism. They were not, as Pipa said, "some idea-driven nationalists." Volodya Ivanov, their manager in those first years, told me that in fact they "had complexes (комплексували), they were ashamed (соромились), because their practice in Ukrainian was not adequate ... But, when they switched to Ukrainian, it was like a defense, it was demonstrative, in some way."[21] Prigova, the producer responsible for getting the "Tantsi" video onto Soviet television, shared her impression of them at the time: "they were searching for their path, they were searching for themselves, for their identity. They wanted to be Ukrainian, but for them it was not clear what that was. They did not speak Ukrainian. They came out on stage and sang in *surzhyk*; in daily life they spoke Russian. There was a bifurcation (роздвоєння) ... that had to be overcome."[22] To overcome it, they leaned hard into the discomfort with non-idiomatic phrases, over-emphatic dialects, and the condescending Russian Imperial and Soviet stereotypes that constructed Ukrainian as a lesser language, and Ukrainians as unsophisticated peasants.

That VV made a deliberate mess of the line between mockery and praise puts them in league with some contemporaries in the Soviet rock scene, such as the Russian

---

[21] Personal interview, January 4, 2022.
[22] Personal interview, January 10, 2022.

groups Zvuki Mu, AVIA, or Nol'. But whereas such groups directed their ambiguously *stiobish* but anti-colonial critiques internally, VV put a specifically Ukrainian spin on the politics of *stiob* in the late Soviet period, voicing their anti-colonial critique through the prism of Russian-Ukrainian relations. Many people wondered then—and some still wonder now—whether VV's techniques of overidentification were meant to belittle Ukrainian language and culture or lift it up as part of an anti-colonial critique.

My account probes this problem in three interdependent registers—archetypal, linguistic, and sonic. Visually (through clothing, imagery, gestures), VV invoked popular late Soviet archetypes of the *zhlob* (redneck), the *sovok* (a variety of the *homo sovieticus*), and the madman—and filtered them through the absurdist theater of punk performance. Lyrically, they milked the ironic potentials of the Ukrainian language, but also merged it with the low-status hybrid Ukrainian-Russian form known as *surzhyk* and the tropes of Soviet official-ese to concoct densely polysemic, often surrealistic, texts that eluded Soviet censorship regimes. Sonically, they drew inspiration from European and US hard rock, new wave, and post-punk groups, Ukrainian folklore, and Soviet state-sanctioned pop music (*estrada*), alchemizing a unique form of Ukrainian punk rock that mocked not only Soviet genres, but also the pompous masculinity of Western rockers. In VV's *Tantsi*, absurdity becomes provocative, and provocation becomes absurd, directed at nothing in particular. The effect: total *stiob*, a riot of half-jokes, winks that might be invitations to collusion, a thick stew of mixed messages that only a humorless academic would ever try to explain.

The *Zhlob,* the Madman, and the *Sovok*: *Stiob* of Archetypes

The original four members of VV made quite an impression visually. The stark discrepancy in height between Pipa and Zdorenko, the plasticity of facial expressions and strange bodily movements, the unusual sartorial choices, the unremarkable hair styles. Writing in 1990, Artemy Troitsky, the dean of Soviet rock journalists, compared Skrypka to Mamonov, the charismatic front man of the Moscow-based band Zvuki Mu: "Oleg is certainly weird on-stage … [he] is driven by crazy Ukrainian small-town folklore."[23] Eugene Hütz remembered the first time he saw Skrypka at the Kyiv Rock Club: "I saw a guy there who completely did not fit this whole punk/metal hang. He had blond hair, and he had an accordion with him, and I was just like 'What the fuck is going on? What is this guy doing here?' … He was kind of eccentric in his own far-out way, in that he looked almost too conservative for this set up."[24] He registered his further shock when he later saw Skrypka join Zdorenko and Pipa—who Hütz knew and admired from their earlier band, SOS—on stage: "This blond dude with the accordion comes out, and I was like, 'what the fuck is he doing with them'"? (As soon as they started to play, Hütz told me, everything suddenly made sense.) But amidst the punks and metalheads with their codified subcultural looks, the musicians of VV seemed odd. Volodymyr Ivanov, VV's manager during their formative years, recalled meeting "Yura (little) and Pipa (big)" the first time they came to his apartment, and

---

[23]Troitskiĭ, *Tusovka : Who's Who in the New Soviet Rock Culture*, 154.
[24]Personal interview, February 3, 2022.

confirmed the same: "They didn't look like the other scenesters (тусовці)." Indeed, through their sartorial choices, hairstyles, gestures, and other visual markers, VV chose not to conform to the dominant subcultural styles, and instead played with several prominent late Soviet archetypes, including the *zhlob*, the madman, and the *sovok*. The Kyiv-based music journalist Yevtushenko later wrote that "the play with comic archetypes of the period, intensified by the national coloring, was achieved best by VV."

And indeed, it was their play with archetypes, it was the juxtaposition and blurring of these boundaries that exposed the banality of each and made their *stiob* of archetypes so effective. Though I briefly turn now to each archetype independently, I insist that these boundaries were deliberately muddied by the members of VV, as they played the cruel stereotypes or absurd assumptions off each other with impertinent nonchalance.

The Zhlob

In the 2013 anthology titled *Zhlobolohia*, the Ukrainian writer and actor Anton Mukharskyi locates the term as originating in mid-nineteenth-century Odesa, when anglophone architects referred to the working-class construction workers who came from the villages to work as "jobbers." According to this etymological story, the term was quickly Slavicized and became "zhlob."[25] Others claim the term as a Yiddish loan word

---

[25]Antin Mukharskyi, *Жлобологія* (Київ: Наш Формат, 2013).; see also Michele Rivkin-Fish, "Tracing Landscapes of the Past in Class Subjectivity: Practices of Memory and Distinction in Marketizing Russia," *American Ethnologist* 36, no. 1 (2009): 92, ftnt 15.

that traveled into mainstream Ukrainian and Russian. In the Soviet period, *zhlobstvo*, or the culture of *zhloby*, became a "term of the totalitarian tradition," and in many contexts, was suggestive of class and ethnic inferiority. *Zhlobstvo* could mark an anxiety about status in relation to state propaganda about the "greatness" of Russia and Russian culture—and the implicit lower status of all other Soviet languages and cultures. According to Michele Rivken-Fish, to be identified as a *zhlob* meant to stand in defiance of Soviet ideals of "kul'turnost," an "elastic concept ... widely accepted as an index of good manners, honesty, education, and decency in interpersonal relation" that was idealized as the backbone of "respectable personhood."[26] The many Ukrainian contributors to *Zhlobolohia* variously define the *zhlob* as a "greedy" person with a "boorish essence," who "wears provincial clothes," "has a limited vocabulary," is "devoid of any spiritual questions or goals." The *zhlob* is a loser, slovenly, often marked as a buffoon who unsuccessfully masks his low-status appetites. A condescending diagnosis, calling someone a *zhlob* implicitly marks the speaker as not-a-*zhlob*.

Zhlobolohia anthologizes and embraces conflicting stories about *zhlobism*. Mukharskyi's introductory essay, titled "*Zhlob. Zhlobstvo. Zhlobism.*," takes pains to acknowledge the contested polysemy of the term. He writes that the "frank polarity of interpretations, the amazing radicalism of differing judgements, the maelstrom of emotions ... all of this allows us to consider the project ambiguous and debatable." But many of the Ukrainian voices featured in *Zhlobolohia* tease out the potential ethnic valences to the culture of *zhlobstvo*. In the USSR, the *zhlob*

---

[26]Rivken-Fish 2009, 83.

became a synecdoche for low-class Soviet citizens; in the mythical Soviet "brotherhood of nations," Ukrainian *zhloby* were the snot-nosed, ignorant, narrow-minded and somewhat embarrassing little siblings—like the characters brought to life in the writings of the Kyivan artist Les Podervianskyi, whose cult *magnitoalbomy* inspired VV's own play with language in the 1980s.[27] Within the Ukrainian space, the *zhlob* was internally displaced, on the margins of the Russified cities, former country bumpkins trying to pass as modern city people. The *zhlob* was, in other words, a lowly Soviet archetype ripe for punk parody.

VV consciously performed Soviet Ukrainian *zhlobstvo*. Russian music journalist Alexander Kushnir's 1999 book, *100 Magnitoalbomy of Soviet Rock, 1977–1991: 15 Years of Underground Recordings*, includes the 1989 *Tantsi* release among more widely circulated Russian Rock albums by Grazhdanskaia Oborona, Kino, Akvarium, DDT, Auction, and others.[28] In this book, Kushnir writes floridly about the impression that VV made, drawing upon the language of *zhlobstvo* to make his point:

> Visually, "VV" presented themselves as a picturesque sight—four *zhloby* from ordinary Borshchahovka [a neighborhood on the south-west outskirts of Kyiv], who, it seems, are about to sing an a cappella hymn to the football exploits of Kyiv's "Dynamo" team. In the corner of the stage, in a beret, with a guitar and bulging eyes, is the former plumber

---

[27]Numerous interviewees who were not in the band mentioned, and later Sashko Pipa confirmed, that Podervianskyi's provocative and often obscene literary experiments in *surzhyk*, which circulated through the Kyivan underground in the early 1980s, exerted a deep influence on the early works of VV.

[28]Alexander Kushnir, *100 Magnitoalbomov Sovetkogo Roka. 1977–1991: 15 Let Podpol'noi Zvukozapysy* (Moscow: Agraf, 1999).

Yuri Zdorenko. Stationed behind Zdorenko is the drummer Serhiy Sakhno, who is bounding like a hare, a student of the Chernobyl dance floors. Beside him, legs wide apart in the heroic pose of a French grenadier, is the lanky Shura Pipa, lips protruding and holding a stumpy bass guitar. His gestures and mocking facial expressions defy description. In the center, at risk of falling into the orchestra pit, the lead singer and button accordionist Oleg Skrypka teeters, as if on a tightrope. Periodically the leader of Vopli plays on the saxophone or trumpet, never forgetting to make the necessary announcement: "Now there will be a solo!" Dressed in the uniform of an unsuccessful thrift shop raider, with circles of black makeup around his eyes, he tempers his demonic image with moves from classical ballet, elements of breakdancing, the lusty hip movements of Jagger and Presley's arsenal, and the clumsy dancing of the village lumpenproletariat. His eyes are ablaze with light.[29]

Such accounts of VV's performance of *zhlobsvto* are widespread, though none that I have found are quite as vivid as Kushnir's description above.

To the Ukrainian rock journalist Oleksandr Yevtushenko, no one embodied the *zhlob* as perfectly as Oleg Skrypka, who exploited "the *surzhyk* of the Kyivan suburbs" and had "the appearance of a typical lumpen-thug." Elena Prigova—the television producer who assembled the panel of experts to provide "political cover" in anticipation that the video would get negative feedback from Soviet censors—told me that the most compelling argument for showing the video was made

[29] This is my original translation from Kushnir's Russian language text.

by the rehabilitated Ukrainian dissident and writer Ivan Dziuba. Dziuba pointed out the universality of the figure of the *zhlob* that was brought to life in the video. For Dziuba, VV's portrayal forced the rueful confrontation with the stereotype of a Ukrainian *zhlob*.[30] Through grotesque overidentification, Dziuba persuaded the panel of experts that "Tantsi" must be shown on Soviet television in order to perform the work of "cleansing, not humiliation."[31] Dziuba, an activist of an older generation, endorsed the video precisely *because* he grasped the display as *stiob*; by appearing as *zhloby*, VV forced the Soviet public to stare head on at the deeply entrenched and dehumanizing stereotype of the low-class Ukrainian hick suffering from an inferiority complex, and contemplate his future place in a rapidly changing society. Performing the *zhlob* might exorcise the demons of inferiority from the Ukrainian polity.

The Madman

By the late 1980s, the madman had become a well-established identity for people living outside of the mainstream of Soviet society. As has been widely documented, dissidents—those whose opposition to the Soviet state was direct and consistent—were often diagnosed with mental illnesses and institutionalized in psychiatric hospitals. But adopting a "politics of madness" became an appealing tactic for other demographics as well. Juliane Fürst, writing about Soviet hippies who longed to exist

---

[30]Michael Herzfeld wrote memorably about the "rueful self-recognition" of the self in national stereotypes in *Cultural Intimacy: Social Poetics in the Nation-State* (2004, 10).
[31]Personal interview with Elena Prigova, January 10, 2022.

outside of the system, explains that "State-declared 'craziness' and the politics surrounding it … emerge as a complex interface between rebellious citizens and their state, between authority and those whose declared ideology it was to deny and ignore this authority … Madness was a weapon as well as a sentence. Craziness meant freedom as well as restraint. Abnormality was a defense as well as an attack." Furthermore, "embracing and celebrating madness were sure signs of anti-Sovietness."[32] Alexei Yurchak's analysis of late Soviet artists offers a slightly different perspective, arguing that the simulation of madness could operate not so much as a sign of "anti-Sovietness" as one of "non-Sovietness," a positioning of oneself entirely outside of the realm of politics. Whether anti- or non-Soviet, acting the madman placed one into a charged relationship to the normative expectations of Soviet citizenship.[33]

VV's adoption of the trope of the madman appears in both archival and ethnographic records. In the band's first known interview in 1988, published in the *samizdat* rock zine *Subjecticon*, for example, Sashko Pipa explained how the band was motivated to put on a display of what seemed too obvious to most: "Our cozy town is amazingly reminiscent of a crazy house. It's just that everyone is used to it and doesn't notice it. It amuses us, and we brought the image of this madman

---

[32] Juliane Fürst, "Liberating Madness–Punishing Insanity: Soviet Hippies and the Politics of Craziness," *Journal of Contemporary History* 53, no. 4 (2018): 836 and 858.

[33] See, for example, Yurchak's discussion of the Russian artists known as the Mit'ki, whose refusal of the available subject positions of "the pro-system 'activist'" or "anti-system 'dissident'" placed them "outside of the boundaries drawn by Soviet authoritative discourse." The aesthetics of *stiob* were also pre-eminent in their practices (Yurchak, *Everything Was Forever, Until It Was No More: The Last Soviet Generation*, 249).

(сумасшедшего) to the stage."[34] Writing in 2011, Yevtushenko wrote about how the VV-led "*stiob*-rock" scene (a term that, he says, became a "domestic substitute for the term 'punk-rock'") made it fashionable to adopt "a healthy, as we thought then, and happy imitation of craziness."[35] And in early 2022, Kyrylo Stetsenko told me about seeing VV perform at the Kyiv Rock Club, being in their thrall, and immediately diagnosing them: "Pipa—paranoid schizophrenic; Skrypka—epileptic; Zdorenko—manic depressive in a manic state." (He didn't offer a diagnosis for Sakhno, the drummer, whom he described as "more modest.") To Stetsenko, VV's performances as madmen reflected to the audience that their own internal madness was a perfectly reasonable reaction to life under the increasingly absurd conditions of late Soviet life.[36]

The Sovok

Sovok is a pejorative slang term related to the *homo sovieticus*, a Soviet sociological construct that depicted dutiful Soviet citizens as brainwashed automatons, stripped of agency. According to Gulnaz Sharafutdinova, the *sovok* was "the more derisive, negative, and colloquial word ... widely used in the late Soviet and post-Soviet periods in reference to Soviet mentality and attitudes of the average Soviet citizen."[37]

---

[34]This 1988 interview is archived on Tatyana Yezhova's blog: https://lehautparleur.livejournal.com/80664.html, accessed February 18, 2022.
[35]Yevtushenko 2011, 51
[36]Personal interview, January 2, 2022.
[37]Gulnaz Sharafutdinova, "Was There a 'Simple Soviet' Person? Debating the Politics and Sociology of '*Homo Sovieticus*,'" *Slavic Review* 78, no. 1 (2019), 182, 194. Importantly, Sharafutdinova's critique is motivated by a sense of urgency, as she perceives the resurgence of the *homo sovieticus*, which has found new purchase in Anglophone discourse since 2016. See also, Krylova, "The Tenacious Liberal Subject in Soviet Studies."

Sharafutdinova indicts the *homo sovieticus*—and, by extension, the *sovok*—as a "deeply conservative" archetype for its "essentialism and deterministic views of individual personality and monolithic culture." For the sociologist Yuri Levada, the originator of the term, the *homo sovieticus* was defined by his "doublethink, flexibility, simplicity, cynicism, and lack of self-respect."[38] Sharafutdinova instead lifts up the work of the Russian sociocultural anthropologist Natalya Kozlova, whose interpretive, ethnographically-grounded approach to studying the everyday lives of late Soviet citizens offers an alternative to the flat caricature of the *homo sovieticus*. Kozlova "viewed individuals as *actors* involved in complex social games and interactive, communicative and discursive processes underpinning the social construction of reality; as *actors* drawing on cognitive devices from publicly available cultural frames and models to form their distinct identities with social meaning and purpose. Her approach allowed for avoiding the duality of structure and agency, and for appreciating both the rules of the game as the structure's listing the range of actions as well as the creative agenda of the players to circumvent the rules as well as stretch, disobey, or apply them creatively."[39] Following from this analysis, then, one can see how VV was participating precisely in a "complex social game" when they performed their overdetermined caricature of the *sovok*—and, in doing so, in Elena Prigova's interpretation, tried to become the generation to finally "break the *sovok*."[40]

The archetype of the *sovok* manifests in VV's output in a few different ways. Visually, the *sovok* was framed by stage elements

---

[38]Ibid, 189.
[39]Ibid., 185.
[40]Personal interview, January 10, 2022.

such as the Soviet agitprop banners and slogans, or indexed through the "proletarian berets" worn by Yuri Zdorenko. But, perhaps most forcefully, the *sovok* comes through in VV's use of language and sound, in the use of Soviet tropes of poetry and melody, and in the utterly platitudinous stage patter Skrypka performed between songs. Perhaps no song from *Tantsi* better captures this than "Buly Den'ki" ("There Were Days"), which I turn to now.[41]

Soviet Speak and Village Vernaculars: Linguistic *Stiob*

My dear city, the city of Kherson,
Nothing is sweeter than you.
White walls of pretty houses,
Balconies on these houses.
And I go, calling to you
To walk until dawn.
And we
Alone
Walk.

The city blooms, like a bouquet.
I gift it to you.

---

[41] It is difficult to convey in translation, but "den'ky" in Ukrainian is a diminutive form of what would otherwise be "dni"—the regular form for "days." With this in mind, the title of the song could be translated as "There Were (Little) Days," but this also fails to capture either the silliness of the original formulation, or the vernacular quality of the phrase, since Ukrainian speakers frequently introduce diminutives into otherwise casual phrases.

Clean plazas, a washed avenue,
Lanterns look upon them.
And we at night, above us are stars,
There is no one anywhere.
And your voice, and the clasp of your hand,
And the first kiss.
Among the trees I gathered my breath,
I stopped you.
I say
To you:
"I love."

There, there, there.
There, there, days.
There, there, there.

My life, my love,
My comrade—Kherson.
Unions, marriages—
In your name . . .[42]

In the early 1990s, a little red book titled "VV Lyrics" was published in Kyiv. It was published by an entity identified as "The Center for Aesthetic Tasting M20" established by Gennady

---

[42]Much nuance gets lost in this translation. Because a word-by-word exegesis is beyond the scope of this chapter, I'll just make the general comment that the lyrics contain several phrases that are non-idiomatic in Ukrainian (дихання зібрав), *surzhyk* terms (любві), and words suggestive of Soviet terminology (товариш). I am grateful to Yuri Shevchuk for helping me decipher some of these elements. A final note: the lyrics here appear as they were performed on the *Tantsi* cassette and in concerts at the time; later recordings of this song have an additional short stanza tacked on as an introduction.

Gutgarts, who worked briefly as a manager for VV, and had been a regular of the Kyiv Rock Club and Rock Artil *tusovkas* in the last Soviet years. The book opens with a fabricated quote from Fyodor Dostoevsky—an irreverent homage to the writer from whom VV took their name. In the little red book, the lyrics of early VV songs are interspersed with black and white photos of the band. It features most of the lyrics for the songs on the 1989 *Fonohraf* release of *Tantsi*, organizing them in chronological order beginning in 1987. "Tantsi" is the first song in the book. The lyrics to "Buly Den'ki" ("There Were Days"), the song translated above, appear on page 39, in the section of lyrics from 1988. When I read the lyrics aloud to Gutgarts during a Zoom interview in early February 2022, he laughed in response to many of the lines. When I finished reading, Gutgarts told me that "Buly Den'ki" sounds like "very refined, intelligent *stiob*."[43]

I concur that "There Were Days" is lyrical *stiob* of the highest order. Written as a parody of a romantic city song—canonical examples of Soviet city songs include "Moscow Nights," "The Bridges of Leningrad," or "The City Over the Wide Neva"— Skrypka's poetry is somewhat ambiguous: is this a love song *to* the city, or a love song *in* a city? Much like the lyrics to the 1957 *estrada* song "The City Over the Wide Neva" (Город над вольной Невой), the protagonist addresses the city as an intimate friend.[44] In "The City Over the Wide Neva," the poetry is acutely Soviet and almost painfully nostalgic: the protagonist reminisces about the places where he met friends, his youth in the Komsomol, the city glorified by the labor of its loving

---

43 Personal interview, February 12, 2022.
44 The song was composed in 1957 by Vasily Soloviev-Sedoy with lyrics by Alexander Churkin. In the 1980s, it was adopted and adapted as the city's unofficial anthem by Leningrad/St. Petersburg football fans.

residents, his restless youth: "Listen, Leningrad, I'll sing to you / My heartfelt song." In Skrypka's "Buly Den'ki," the poetry is, in contrast, strangely generic, praising white walls, a washed avenue, and lanterns, and then shifting towards bloated rhetorical flourishes: "The city blooms like a bouquet / I gift it to you." Or take the overzealous couplet towards the end: "My life, my love / My comrade—Kherson."

Kherson is a southern Ukrainian port city known in Soviet times as a ship-building hub, and Skrypka told me that he chose Kherson "because it was funny."[45] When he wrote "There Were Days," he had never been to Kherson, but "it was a statistically average Soviet city. If Gogol once wrote about provincial town M, Kherson was provincial town N: with Khrushchovkas (хрущовки)—these five-story blocks of buildings—and in the middle a statue of Lenin, some kind of park, a healthy-sized plaza laid with concrete slabs, and these kinds of Soviet prospect. And that's why there's this image; but the song is about love."[46] Delighted at the longevity of the song's success, Skrypka chuckled as he told me that the song is treated by some as "the unofficial hymn of Kherson." I asked him if it had been adopted seriously, and he responded with a shrug: impossible to know. With *stiob*, after all, not being able to tell is part of the point. I asked Gutgarts a version of this question too, and he answered that it was "narrowly

---

[45]Kherson takes on different resonances in 2022, since it was the first city to be occupied by the Russian army in early March of 2022, though reportage from within the city showed a sustained refusal to submit to Russian rule. On November 11, 2022, Kherson was liberated from Russian occupation by the Ukrainian Armed Forces (ZSU). That evening, my social media feeds were flooded with videos of people in Kherson partying on the streets in celebration; VV's 1989 video of "Buly Den'ki" was also being shared widely.
[46]Personal interview, June 5, 2019.

understood" as parody—only specific individuals oriented to the politics of *stiob* would have gotten the joke. His father, he told, would not have understood it, but Soviet rock scenesters "understood everything."

If "There Were Days" is "refined, intelligent *stiob*" that parodies sentimental urban Soviet song forms, then "Tantsi" and the related song "Pisenk'a" is *stiob* that parodies Soviet stereotypes of Ukrainian rurality and the dutiful *sovok* who exists unproblematically within the system. In "Tantsi," as I described in the introduction to this book, the workers who are "tired of working" dream earnest dreams about dancing their favorite dances on the weekend at the "club." Skrypka characterized the style of the "Tantsi" lyrics to me as "Dadaist," though he "only learned about the Dadaists" after the fact. When I asked Skrypka to tell me more about what I assumed to be a mythical club in "Tantsi," his answer surprised me:

> These were not mythical dances. There was a specific club (конкретний клуб) which I visited in the village … This is the village Hil'tsi, Poltava oblast', Chornohirskyi region. And in the center of this village, near the store, near the village administration building, this club still exists. And when I was in my grandfather's village I would go to this club for dances. And so, this atmosphere, in principle, was transmitted.[47]

This same club is featured in another popular song from the *Tantsi* era: "Pisen'ka," or "Little Song." In the little red book of lyrics, it follows "Tantsi" in the 1987 section, and a lyric from the song gave the name to the *samizdat* magazine *Huchnomovets*

---

[47]The village is about a three-hour drive eastward from the capital city of Kyiv.

described in Chapter two. But Pisen'ka was not one of the fourteen tracks included in the 1989 *Fonohraf* release. It was, however, recorded during the same session, and is featured as a digital extra on the remastered release paired to the publication of this book. And, as Skrypka pointed out to me, the music video that accompanied the post-Soviet studio release of "Pisen'ka" is set in the village of Hil'tsi and shows that lineup of VV performing to the villagers outside of the very same club in the center of town.

VV's performance of "Pisen'ka" in 1988 at the Moscow SyROK festival is archived on YouTube by the person who runs the Retro.vv blog.[48] The clip is valuable also because it includes an example of Skrypka's stage patter at the time. When he introduces "Tantsi," Skrypka speaks to the audience in a calm and authoritative tone, explaining, "We play about life, about us with you, about this audience, about rock, about our life, about *perebudova*. And so, in other words, I want to say . . . " and he segues into the opening lyrics of "Tantsi," at which point his voice shifts register and his pronunciation mimics the exaggerated Poltavan dialect described earlier. The clip then cuts to VV's performance of "Pisen'ka," which has the feel of a blues-rock shuffle led by Skrypka's melodies on bayan.

The lyrics of "Pisen'ka" merge rural imagery with aphorisms attributed to the singers' grandfather ("that which does not bloom will wither" and "Don't trample the grass near the house, Hryts, don't do it"). The chorus is raucous and involves a lot of crowd-pleasing "Ohs"! and "Heys." In the context of the song, these sayings are quite out of place—the reference to Hryts, which is a nickname for Hryhorii (Gregory), is a trope of

---

[48]Video available at https://www.youtube.com/watch?v=fVG-YJZe4Sw, accessed February 19, 2022.

Ukrainian folk songs: in different songs, Hryts mows the grass, or courts a milk maid, or carries water, etc. The inclusion of Hryts in this song is *stiob*. The rousing chorus of the song describes the boys playing near the city administration building, and how they are not allowed to enter the club because they are "very shaggy." The word Skrypka uses here—"патлаті"—is a colloquial term suggestive of rurality. In sum, the song quilts together unexpected elements: the juxtaposition of Soviet village attributes with folkloric flourishes, packaged together in a bayan-forward blues-rock jam. VV's 1988 live performance further underscores the tonal instability in the song, as the placid blues rock moments are disrupted by heavy distorted guitars, and as the more conversational singing style of the verses shifts towards pleading punk rock screams on the word "Mamo." Towards the end of the song, the phrase "the boys play as loudspeakers!" ("хлопці грають в гучномовець!") is sung on an ascending arpeggiated chord that breaks with the melodic elements that preceded it. It begs for an audience to sing along (and was, in fact, the line that inspired the name for the *samizdat* zine *Huchnomovets*).

In both song texts described above, and in many of the nine Ukrainian-language tracks on *Tantsi*, Skrypka sings with a noticeable accent, often employs non-standard words in the low-status hybrid Ukrainian-Russian linguistic form known as *surzhyk*, and shifts—often rapidly—between language highly suggestive of "authoritative" Soviet speak and stereotypically folklorized rural Ukrainian. Skrypka told me that he started experimenting with the regional "Poltavan" accent in Zdorenko's kitchen, where they recorded the first VV demos: "It was then that I started to experiment with the Ukrainian language, layered with a Poltavan accent—I think it's genetic for me— over rock riffs." (Others, such as Oleksandr Rudiachenko, heard

Skrypka's unusual dialect as imitating the speech of Ukrainians in the Canadian diaspora, but when I asked Skrypka about this, he rejected this interpretation flatly, claiming that he would have had absolutely no exposure to Canadian-Ukrainian speech in the mid-1980s.)

Both Pipa and Skrypka frequently told me that they preferred Ukrainian because it was more melodious, more suitable to song lyrics, and "it sounded cool." Both also insisted that their usage of the language came from a place of respect, but separately described how fully inculcated they were, at the time, in the belief that the Russian language was the language of youth, and of the future. Laada Bilaniuk, in her stellar ethnographic study of language practices in post-Soviet Ukraine, described a similar uneasy concurrence of love and disdain for the Ukrainian language: "A woman in the western Ukrainian city of Ivano-Frankivs'k once told me that 'the villages saved the [Ukrainian] language,' and a minute later she spoke of the 'awful village language.' I was stunned by the close coexistence of such contradictory views in her thinking: the romanticized ideal of the village versus the village as lacking culture."[49] Similarly, Yuri Shevchuk, who coined the provocative term "linguistic schizophrenia" to describe Ukrainians' attitudes to language politics, notes the "stigma of provincialism" that marked the Ukrainian language. He writes about the Russian Imperial historical campaign that began in the early eighteenth century and aimed to "reduc[e Ukrainian] to a pale simulacrum of the 'great and mighty Russian language.'" For Shevchuk, such "symbolic violence ... amount[s] to linguicide." He then enumerated the ways in which Russification policies inhibited

---

[49]Laada Bilaniuk, *Contested Tongues: Language Politics and Cultural Correction in Ukraine* (Ithaca, NY: Cornell University Press, 2005), 119.

Ukrainian from developing the "processes that make a language dynamic, prestigious, and attractive for those who speak it."[50]

Even if we allow for the possibility that aspects of VV's use of language could be enacting forms of (internal or external) Ukrainophobia, VV's experimental uses of Ukrainian nonetheless made the language seductive to a young generation of rock fans who sang along with the linguistic *stiob* that laughed at itself while it pilloried historical stereotypes of Ukrainian backwardness.

Punk Heroics and Ambiguous Influence: Sonic and Gestural *Stiob*

Unlike the lyrical and archetypal dimensions of VV's songs and performances—which parodied Ukrainian and Soviet-specific genres through overidentification—the sound of VV's music expanded the territory of *stiob* to include Western rock music cultures. Yes, they were skewering the saccharine and proper culture of state-sanctioned Soviet pop music, or *estrada*, but they were also mocking the self-indulgent tropes of 1970s hard rock. Deflating the peacocking guitar hero, VV placed themselves in league with some Western European and American post-punk bands of the late 1970s and 1980s, a la Devo's 1978 de-sexed robotic cover of the Rolling Stones' "Satisfaction." The so-called "Imaginary West" described by Yurchak in *Everything Was Forever, Until It Was No More* appears

---

[50]Yuri I. Shevchuk, *Ukrainian-English Collocation Dictionary* (New York: Hippocrene Books, 2021), ix–x.

here not *only* as a site of desire, but also as an unexplored terrain for *stiob*-ish inspiration.

The driving rock riff of "There Were Days" provides acoustic evidence for this claim. In 2019, Oleg Skrypka described the "dust-covered guitar sound" in the blues-rock song, and then compared the angular riff upon which the song is built to the "Soviet Khatchaturian heroic style." Singing, he imitated this heroic style for me in the interview—*ta dY ta DYY, ta dY ta DYYY*! Skrypka's sung mimicry was accompanied by broad gestures that evoked, for me, images of mid-century propaganda about the miraculous productivity of Soviet workers, perhaps miners from Donbas. Reminiscing about the silliness of the riff, Skrypka said, "There was some Soviet TV program with a similar melody—a heroic one. It makes you want to pour out steel, to do something like that to this music."[51] Indeed, the chunky propulsive rhythm of the opening riff conjures monumentality. It is therefore no surprise that, when VV performed "Buly Den'ki" for a French TV documentary on Soviet rock in 1989, recorded in Moscow, they chose as their setting one of the most iconic architectural sites of high Stalinism: The Exhibition of the Achievements of the National Economy Park (VDNKh), opened in 1939 to reward the Soviet population for their progress in modernization.[52]

In the video, the members of VV are encircled by a crowd of mild-mannered Muscovites as images cut between the Stakhanovite figures who carry a basket of grain on the high point of the arch, and the faces of each member of VV. Their faces telegraph awe, but with a wink. The riff takes off, and

---

[51]Personal interview, June 5, 2019.
[52]The video can be viewed at: https://youtu.be/7Mu_Ilf7E1A (last accessed February 23, 2022).

Figure 3.1A *Zdorenko against the monumental backdrop of VDNKh*

Figure 3.1B *Pipa rocks out on bass*

Figure 3.1D *Skrypka leans into the audience*

Figure 3.1C *Skrypka leaps while Zdorenko poses*

Skrypka—dressed in all-black with a red carnation in his breast pocket—starts to bounce on his toes, singing his love song for Kherson. Like an unhinged magician, he conjures from his pocket the bright red ribbon of a rhythmic gymnast and dashes around the circle of watchers, twirling and leaping with accelerating speed. Skrypka's frenzied parody of heroism matches the sonic environment of the song, which centers on the perennial repetition of the "Soviet Khatchaturian heroic style."

But there is another reference baked into this infectious riff: melodically and structurally, it is a near copy of the Golden Earring's 1973 hit song "Radar Love."[53] The same notes appear,

---

[53]"Radar Love" can be viewed at: https://youtu.be/aRISHG5hRY4—the riff enters at :29. I am grateful to Franz Nicolay for hearing this connection.

even in the same key (G), in nearly identical patterns of repetition. But where the VV riff is angular and square, the Golden Earring riff is lighter, with a shuffle-feel. I asked Sashko Pipa whether this borrowing was intentional, and he told me that he was not aware of the song "Radar Love." Skrypka offered only the reference to the "heroic Soviet style" discussed above. So, what do we make of this? Could it be coincidence, or could we hear this borrowing—perhaps unintentional, but nonetheless audible—as a kind of Western-oriented *stiob*? Intentionally or not, Zdorenko's guitar repurposes the riff of "Radar Love." In a world of not taking anything too seriously—"especially rock," as Zdorenko claimed in the epigraph to this chapter—I hear this riff as yet another signal of VV's irreverent attitude towards *everything*: to the pieties of Western rock music, the blurred lines of influence versus inspiration, and the panic of Soviet ideologues rushing to stamp out Soviet youth's infatuation with rock music through bungling techniques of control.

Recall that the Soviet war on rock had begun at least five years before VV's love song to Kherson aired on French television. Multiple articles condemning the corrupting sound of rock resorted to scientistic language documenting "the insidious effects of low frequencies, loud volumes, and distorted sounds of Western rock bands on the human psyche."[54] Such fear-mongering imagery only emboldened VV, who were savvy enough to play two angles at once: first, they could strike fear in the heart of Soviet ideologues by showing that they had, in fact, been irredeemably corrupted by the sounds of rock—they were madmen, after all. Second, they could mock the pompousness and earnestness of the Western 1970s hard rock that had

---

[54]Yurchak 2005, 227.

purportedly ruined them. If conventional Cold War narratives emphasize the longing of Soviet subjects for the freedoms of the capitalist West, the sonic *stiob* of VV suggests that the extravagances of the so-called "free world" were also not spared from satirical overidentification. Despite their performance as unsophisticated rubes, VV were in fact skilled parodists targeting not only the overdetermined genres of Soviet language, archetype, and musical form, but also the sanctimonious promise of the capitalist West.

I will end this chapter with a question inspired by this VV album from 1989 but heartbreakingly relevant to the brutal politics of 2022: through their total *stiob*, might we understand the art of these late Soviet Ukrainian punk rockers as activating a nascent politics of Ukrainian sovereignty—a clear-eyed refusal of the status quo in the socialist political economic order as well as in the capitalist one, as a determination to make something outside of these systems? At an ironic remove, certainly, but keenly engaged and rightfully critical.

4 Sex, Drugs, and Komsomol

This chapter is neither about sex nor drugs, but it is about the Komsomol. It is about how the hedonistic spirit of rock and roll captured in the cliche of "sex, drugs, and rock and roll" clashed against the buttoned-up soft police regime of the Komsomol (Communist Youth League) apparatchiks, and the more muscular enforcement strategies of the KGB. To borrow from Kyrylo Stetsenko, this is a story about "how to be effective in a moment of obstruction." It is about when the new freedoms of the late 1980s clashed with earlier Soviet cultures of control, when attempts to keep the lid on Soviet nonconformist youth, the *neformaly* whose social lives revolved around rock music subcultures, started to spill out of the underground and into the mainstream of late Soviet society. Musical expressions, of course, are notoriously ambiguous, dense with slippery meaning. Unlike purely visual or literary forms, the simultaneous polysemy of music—which can encode multiple ambiguous symbols in sound as well as in textual, and often visual-gestural registers—was a powerful tool used to gum up ham-fisted techniques of regulation.

This chapter is also about the problem that rock and roll posed to existing Soviet musical institutions. Moral panic over the degradation of youth was a through-line of post-war popular culture in the USSR (as in the US, where many of these youth trends originated). In the Soviet case, the trajectory from

Figure 4.1 *A badge honoring the sixtieth anniversary of the Soviet Ukrainian Komsomol. From the author's personal collection.*

1940s to 1950s *stilyagi* (Soviet hipsters), to late-1960s hippies, to late-1970s hard rockers, to mid-1980s punk rockers, shadowed the generational trends marked by shifts in Anglo-American popular (especially musical) subcultures. Although these Soviet subcultures may have been small, and looked upon by the majority "with disdain," they were "nonetheless a symptom of a much bigger emerging importance of Westernized imaginations among millions of regular Soviet youths."[1]

Tantsi

[1]Yurchak 2005, 170.

The 1980s presented the most serious threat to Soviet regimes of subcultural control, as music seeped across Cold War borders more seamlessly than before with the advent of cassette dubbing technologies, and Gorbachev's reforms allowed young people greater freedoms of mobility and expression. Volodya Ivanov wrote to me that "in conservative Soviet circles there was a long-standing campaign against rock music and other youth subcultures under the shared slogan 'Rock–a plague of the 20th century!'"[2] Sergei Zhuk has written extensively about the panic over "fascist punks" among Komsomol activists and police in the closed city of Dnipropetrovsk (now Dnipro). There, the Komsomol and KGB frequently conflated "punk" with "fascism," failing to identify "one fashionable hairstyle from another or distinguish between 'hard rock' and 'punk rock'" (152). Zhuk details how the wry British pop-rock group 10cc, for example, came to be placed on the list of "pro-fascist, anti-Soviet bands" for their "hellish, anti-human imagery, fascist symbols, and anti-Soviet lyrics:"

> [10cc] was mistakenly re-interpreted as "Ten SS," referring to Hitler's secret police, the SS (Schutzstaffel). Given that the English letter "c" is the equivalent of the letter "s" in Russian and Ukrainian, cc (cubic centimeters) was pronounced "ess-ess," and local Komsomol ideologists immediately characterized 10cc as a "fascist name." Moreover, the band's 1978 album *Bloody Tourists* included a musical parody of the anti-Soviet hysteria experienced during the Cold War entitled "Reds in My Bed." The refrain of this song shocked the Soviet censors: "I've got Reds in my bed, I'm not easily led to the slaughter, and while the Cold War exists, I'll stay warm with the Commissar's

---

[2]Personal correspondence, January 4, 2022.

daughter … Let me go home. You're a land full of misery. I
don't like your philosophy. You're a cruel and faceless race."[3]

Local Komsomol leaders—missing the joke completely with
their flat-footed literalism, and in concert with the local KGB—
worked assiduously to ban the music of 10cc and many other
misunderstood bands from the Dnipropetrovsk discotheques
in the early 1980s.

But only a few years later, in Kyiv, when VV had their home-
grown variety of ironic punk rock vetted by Komsomol
committees, they usually passed through with only minor
hurdles. Of course, restrictions on expression were loosening
after the Central Committee of the USSR launched its programs
of *uskorennia* (acceleration) and *perebudova* (restructuring) in
April 1985. But the critical point, according to Oleg Skrypka,
was simply that the "Komsomol didn't understand our music,
didn't understand that it was sarcastic"[4]—that it was pushing
the envelope with its total Ukrainian *stiob*.

Kyrylo Stetsenko, whose decades-long career as a musician
and media personality was marked by instances of censorship
and black-listing, put it this way: "the KGB did not understand
non-verbal modes of communication. They could not hear
past the old technologies of communication … they could not
hear what lay under the text." Stetsenko recounted how he
came into awareness that, through "style rather than text," he

---

[3]Sergei I. Zhuk, "Fascist Music from the West: Anti-Rock Campaigns, Problems of
National Identity, and Human Rights in the 'Closed City' of Soviet Ukraine,
1975–84," in *Popular Music and Human Rights: Volume II: World Music* ed. Ian
Peddie (London: Routledge, 2011), 152. Yurchak (2005, 214–15) reproduces the
full list of harmful bands designated by the Ukrainian Komsomol, and also
acknowledges how lyrics were interpreted literally, in opposition to how
Soviet youth were consuming them.
[4]Personal interview, June 5, 2019.

could communicate subversive messages even while he was being monitored by the KGB. As a teenager spending a summer with his grandmother in Poland in 1970, Stetsenko became enamored with the fast and punchy verbal style of the popular hosts on Radio Luxembourg. When, years later, he hosted his first radio show, "Musical Contrasts" (Музичні Контрасти)— a "self-justifying name" that allowed him to play anything he wanted, he told me—Stetsenko "wanted to unite the most lively and sharp ways to talk to people via the radio in order to show that what was Ukrainian was in the future, and not the past. In other words, to change the image of Ukraine, that it is not just old guys living in the past, but about young people who are still to come." And so, understanding that the KGB was listening in, he "tried to influence people non-verbally": through his intonation, by where he placed emphasis, through the unconventional vocabulary he used; and, of course, through the music he chose to showcase.[5] He described it as "playing a game to be able to do what you want, but also to be able to *continue* to do it. It was a balancing act."

For musicians coming of age in the second half of the 1980s, there were two major roadblocks they might confront (depending on the month, and the direction of the political wind) before they could bring their music to the stage: *litovannia* (літовання), the formal registration of texts that—when adapted from literary to musical contexts—took the form of a dress rehearsal performed in front of a panel of Komsomol and other apparatchiks; and *taryfikatsia* (тарифікація), a form of accreditation that conferred status upon musicians as either "professional" or "amateur," with finer-grained divisions in the professional tier enabling

---

[5]Personal interview, January 2, 2022.

Sex, Drugs, and Komsomol

musicians access to different kinds of performance opportunities and compensation structures.

Many people I interviewed also spoke about the near-ubiquitous presence of KGB (in Ukrainian, KDB, or КДБ) operatives at various rock concerts and festivals in that period, but they had little disruptive effect. KGB types—who stood out by their age, dress, and demeanor—would most often be politely noted and ignored. Rockers would witness men-in-suit types observing keenly, maybe even taking notes. Everyone understood there would be a report filed somewhere, but there was little fear at this moment in Soviet history that there would be consequences of any gravity.

Moving through the procedures of *litovannia* and *taryfikatsia*, however, meant directly encountering Komsomol leaders and navigating through trials of censorship and standards of professionalism. Here is it important to mark a distinction between Komsomol leaders—many of whom maintained the system without irony—and rank-and-file Komsomol members. The vast majority of young people of VV's generation were at least nominally members of the Komsomol, because Komsomol membership meant access: to higher education; to employment; to resources such as rehearsal space, guitars, and amplifiers; and to opportunities—performances at official Komsomol-operated Rock Clubs, foreign tours, media exposure. Being in the Komsomol allowed daily life to be lived with less friction. And it was through the Komsomol, according to Yurchak, that "members of that generation became routinely exposed to authoritative discourse,"[6] the very same discourse that VV so fluidly parodied

---

[6]Yurchak 2005, 287.

in their impudent punk rock. Komsomol true believers, on the other hand, were a "very specific" kind of people, according to Oleg Skrypka. Comfortable in their positions of authority, they were as often as not unmoved by Communist party ideology, but were rather people who did what they needed to do to secure the social and political benefits that came with their leadership positions.

In numerous conversations with former participants in the Kyiv rock scene, the Komsomol apparatchiks of the 1980s were regarded with the equivalent of an eye roll.[7] But the Komsomol were both the enablers and the antagonists of the Kyiv Rock underground: even if you disdained them, you had to deal with them. As rock bands proliferated in the Soviet 1980s, inviting high-level discussions among various musical institutions about how to address "the problem of rock and roll," the unlikely alliance of the Komsomol with the smart-alecky hedonists of the rock scene solidified. VV, who were emerging just as the Komsomol-sponsored Kyiv Rock Club came into being, were no exception.

The Problem of Rock and Roll

In early April of 1988, the Union of Composers of Ukraine held a plenum on the topic of "The World, Music, and Youth" in Kyiv

---

[7]Personal interview with Skrypka, June 5, 2019. Yurchak (2005) insists that Komsomol leaders could also participate in *stiob* and maintain a cognitive dissonance between their personal ideological beliefs ("they believed in Communism") and their performative relationship to official rituals and authoritative discourse (259–64). Although this may be true, the individuals interviewed from this project drew very clear lines between themselves and the Komsomol leaders with whom they had to interact.

that dwelled heavily on "the problem of rock and roll."[8] Thirteen organizations took part, including the Komsomol of Ukraine, the newly formed Kyivan collective "Experiment" (under whose umbrella Rock Artil had begun to sponsor rock concerts two months earlier), in addition to the Union of Ukrainian Composers, the Ministry of Culture of the Ukrainian Soviet Socialist Republic, and the Kyiv City Jazz Club. The transcript from that meeting, which I was able to access in the CSAMM Archive in Kyiv in 2019, began with the words of Comrade O.D. Trybushnyi, the Deputy Minister of Culture of the Ukrainian SSR. Trybushnyi outlines what he views as the deficiencies in aesthetic education in Soviet Ukrainian musical institutions. He also defends the Ministry of Culture from accusations of ineffectiveness that he feels are unjust, and admonishes educational and vocational institutions of music to bring more initiative to the re-invigoration of Ukrainian musical culture, "because of course water does not run under a sleeping stone."[9] His speech set the charged tone—there are serious problems, and we must solve them—after which numerous others followed.

The very next speaker was Taras Mel'nyk of the Kyiv Conservatory (who would go on, in the following year, to found the Chervona Ruta festival of Ukrainian rock music, a watershed event in twentieth-century Ukrainian musical

---

[8]The fact that such "problems" could be so openly discussed lines up with the Union-wide acceleration of *glasnost* that followed the removal of the Politburo conservative Yegor Ligachev—who was widely believed to want to "keep ideological censorship in place"—from his position in charge of state media in March 1988. As Zubok writes, "From then on, *glasnost* progressed by leaps and bounds." Vladislav A. Zubok, *Collapse: The Fall of the Soviet Union* (New Haven: Yale University Press, 2021), 40.
[9]CSAMM, f. 661, op. 1, d. 1477, pp. 6; The archival holding can be viewed at: https://csamm.archives.gov.ua/.

history in which VV also took part). Mel'nyk began his speech from the premise that "the system of musical education is not working." He asks, "Whom do we want to educate, and on what?" Over the course of what must have been at least a twenty-minute speech (it is ten pages in the transcript, with two musical examples indicated), Mel'nyk strongly criticizes the music curriculum that was apparently being proposed for schoolchildren. The proposed curriculum had been adapted from Dmitri Kabalevsky's earlier program, and Mel'nyk castigates it for being "outdated and backwards-looking." Instead, he argues, "we must look ahead, at what will come next, and in what way." He warns that by believing that the status quo is sufficient, the assembled music workers of Ukraine risk everything: "We may be seated on a powder keg that could tear the whole culture apart." Mel'nyk then advances suggestions to prevent this explosion by emphasizing the two genres whose trajectories he views as most promising: folklore and rock.

First, Mel'nyk asks the audience to rethink how folklore is introduced and taught to young people. In the current system, folk musics are introduced after classical music. "Where is the logic in this"? he asks. "There is none." Mel'nyk posits that the old "Stalinist folklore aesthetic … where people only dance, rejoice, and have fun" denies the Ukrainian public any of the psychological depth—the drama, tragedy, and specific history that should be embedded in traditional music. He warns that "if we do not give the youth this, all of them will leave us." He continues to say that the ossified folk aesthetic does not draw crowds because it is so superficial: "there is nothing alive in it for the soul." His diatribe against the abuse of folklore ends with a series of questions that become his pivot to more problems: "Do we really think that there are no genres that could help us in thinking about our history and our social problems? Here it is, the problem."

The problem with rock, according to Mel'nyk, is dire. It is as urgent, he believed, as the quest for a national compositional style was for nineteenth-century composers. Mel'nyk argues that both rock and pop music "must adapt to our social conditions and nationalize from the perspective of music. Otherwise, it will not fit; it will ruin our culture. We must create now, immediately, a national school of rock and pop music." Despite being an import from the US, he says, rock nonetheless performs a "social and critical function." To Mel'nyk, "rock is needed, it bears fruit." He muses out loud about the question of whether it "proposes some higher ideals"—conceding that this is unclear—but because it depicts life as it is, rock has undeniable value. For the benefit of an audience that he knows to be skeptical of a pro-rock position, he describes what rock music culture is, adopting a didactic tone:

> Now, rock music is made up of many components. Apart from the text and the language, no one can deny, there is a scenography, behavior on the stage, the image, symbolism, attributes—this is the staged componentry.
>
> And then there is the musical componentry ... which includes also many elements. Let's begin with its attributes and symbols—tell me, which of these comes from Soviet reality?
>
> Mostly it's all borrowed from the West.

But there is one Ukrainian rock group whom Mel'nyk believes has innovated an authentic Ukrainian rock style: VV. He says, "I'm not against borrowing, but only one group leads ... Indeed, this group really led our reality. It was a shock, to be honest; this was bold and good, I would say. Here is this grotesque, ironic depiction of dances at the village club. For the first time on the rock stage, our reality was shown." Mel'nyk sees the future in VV's twisted display in "Tantsi." (When I read this archival transcript from 1988 anew in the spring of 2022 as I was drafting this chapter, I gasped.)

Mel'nyk advances the thesis that a successful Ukrainian youth music must develop such a fresh "manner of intonation (інтонування)." Here he invokes a key term of Soviet musicology. The theory of intonation was introduced by the Soviet Russian musicologist Boris Asafyev in the 1940s, and has been defined by Izaly Zemtsovsky "as a function of social consciousness, which always comes into existence in a tripartite act of creation, execution (i.e., reproduction), and perception."[10] J. Martin Daughtry offers the following definition: "Asafyev uses the word 'intonation' (intonatsia) to refer to a complex and dynamic phenomenon that comprises a musical gesture or combination of gestures, its performance or 'articulation,' and the semantic charge (i.e., the meaningful content) that the gesture carries. This charge is ascribed to the musical gesture by the historically situated group of performers and listeners that produce and receive it."[11] To prove his point about the need for new intonations, Mel'nyk proceeded to offer two musical excerpts that embodied distinct types of intonation for the assembled plenary public. Unfortunately, the archival transcript does not include details on the examples Mel'nyk played, but he does

---

[10]Izaly Zemtsovsky, "Musicological Memoirs on Marxism," in *Music & Marx: Ideas, Practice, Politics*, ed. Regula Burckhardt Qureshi (New York and London: Routledge, 2002), 184.

[11]J. Martin Daughtry, "Russia's New Anthem and the Negotiation of National Identity," *Ethnomusicology* 47, no. 1 (2003).

tell his audience that he has chosen examples that are not rock, but nonetheless "absolutely apply to all styles, including rock."

Mel'nyk concludes his impassioned remarks with a rousing call to action directed to the Komsomol. The stakes are clear to him, and extremely high—the imagery of a Cold War arms race is transposed in his closing argument about music, perhaps as a rhetorical strategy to inflame the old guard of composers most entrenched in the status quo. His message is clear: this is war, and we are losing.

Mel'nyk's historic speech has not, to my knowledge, previously appeared in translation. I therefore offer his concluding argument at length, which I translated from the original Ukrainian:

> We will never catch up, we will never compete with [the US] in the forms, these genres, that arose over there. And is it necessary to do so? Isn't our civilization, our culture capable of developing its own building blocks of music, which are based perhaps in other social principles, where humans occupy a central place, where culture is national, where our emotions play an important role.
>
> This is our historical task, and it is a decisive one, to which we will return—this is what we will face in the twenty-first century. Just as these tasks appeared in the nineteenth century. Now is the crucial moment. Are our young amateur creators capable of understanding that they are just a secondary phenomenon, that they are simply imitating what has been said for a long time, and that they cannot achieve anything new?
>
> I think that we must appeal to the Central Committee of the Komsomol on behalf of the Conservatory to create a

laboratory of contemporary instrumental music, which could try through its forms and genres to produce intonations that correspond to us, which are native to us. Otherwise, we cannot compete with them, because in America and in other countries there are institutions working on this, and they are already influencing young people here, and are already launching into production.

And meanwhile, we just wave our hands. If we do not make such a laboratory, we will not be able to find our way in the history of art.[12]

The transcript indicates applause at this moment. The following speaker, V. S. Symonenko, praised Mel'nyk's speech and compared rock culture to a "genie we let out of a bottle," which no matter "how primitive," has found a devoted audience and therefore must be treated as a problem that can be solved. Symonenko, the director of the Ukrainian branch of the Central Musical Forum of the USSR (Центрмузінфорум СК СРСР) and a historian of jazz, diagnoses the problem of rock as a matter of rudderlessness—someone must take responsibility for rock music, bring it into conformity with the expectations of the existing institutions. He suggests stricter measures to vet the professionalism and quality of rock musicians in Ukraine, and to ensure the felicitous synthesis of rock music with Ukrainian national style.

What is striking—if not surprising, given the venue—is the degree to which solutions to the "problem of rock" imagine a future in which rock culture becomes domesticated, housed within the Conservatory, integrated into the elite hierarchies

---

[12]CSAMM, f. 661, op. 1, d. 1477, pp. 7–17.

upon which the Union of Composers was premised. Even Mel'nyk, the great defender of rock, envisions it elevated and legitimized within the Conservatory. Symonenko, and many speakers who followed him in the 1988 plenum, suggest other ways to inscribe the rock music subculture into existing institutional paradigms. They resolve to hold a meeting with representatives of the Kyivan *neformaly* later that year, to hear their concerns, and strategize about how to better incorporate them into the institutions of Soviet music. Volodya Ivanov, who participated in that conversation as a token *neformal*—he felt like an "exotic bird," he recalled—remembered how absurd it felt to walk over to the hallowed assembly hall of the Union of Composers, as though his activities could somehow be reconciled with the procedures and rituals of musical officialdom.

And indeed, none of the speakers at the Plenum seem to consider that the very same Kyivan rock musicians praised by Mel'nyk for perfecting a vernacular Ukrainian rock were simultaneously, in their blithe way, intensifying the crisis that the institutionalists were trying to solve. No one commented on the idea that the rockers might be willing to comply with systems of control for purely opportunistic reasons. With a burlesqued wink, VV found methods of compliance that passed through blunt systems of control without being unduly compromised by them; and in fact, used those systems of control to ridicule existing institutional paradigms of musical expression. Even techniques of regulation such as *litovannia* and *taryfikatsia* backfired because they became ludicrous limits against which VV could push, catalyzing their creativity in reactive ways.

Litovannia: A Ritual of Censorship

Litovannia was a procedural form of censorship originally developed to regulate and legalize Soviet literary texts before publication. *Litovannia* was conducted by the organ of censorship known as Glavlit (Главлит in Russian), an abbreviation for the "Main Directorate for the Protection of State Secrets in the Press and other Mass Media," established in 1918. Glavlit censors were tasked with scrubbing texts of elements that might embarrass the Soviet state, reveal internal dissent, or threaten powerful institutions and individuals. Though censorship practices changed with political orders over the course of eight decades of Soviet rule, it was consistently true that Glavlit censors had limited tolerance for language uses that were abstract, satirical, or experimental, and that they applied blunt tools to weed out anything that could be potentially subversive. "Glavlit's judgements," wrote Richard Sakwa, "had been regulated by no proclaimed laws or procedures, and its decisions had been arbitrary."[13] Though its censorship function was loosened with Gorbachevian *glasnost* reforms starting in June 1986, the vetting of official books, magazines, film scripts, poems, and more continued (in slightly different forms) until the dissolution of the USSR. The *litovannia* of song texts in the Ukrainian SSR, according to numerous individuals interviewed for this project, continued in Kyiv until the middle of 1988.

Procedures of *litovannia* related awkwardly to contexts of musical performance. The application of *litovannia* to non-state sanctioned music seems to have begun in the 1960s,

---

[13]Sakwa, *Gorbachev and His Reforms (1985–1990)*, 67.

with the advent of Soviet "bards" whose original songs (авторські пісні [Ukr]) employed sophisticated poetic techniques, often to code criticism of Soviet state power.[14] Classified as "amateur" (самодіяльні) musicians by Soviet rubrics, bards did not have access to the big professional stages of the Soviet Union that were controlled by the institutional creative unions of composers or writers.[15] But the bards drew crowds of mostly young people, and *magnitizdat*— illicit cassette recordings—of their apartment concerts (квартирники) circulated widely in intellectual and youth circles.[16] The threat posed by these amateur songwriters to the monopolistic creative unions—whose remit was limited to the regulation of elite professional artists—was therefore concrete. And so, beginning in the mid-1970s, the Komsomol appealed to amateur songwriters with a deal: in exchange for some degree of Komsomol oversight, these musicians could finally get access to some of the equipment (microphones, amplifiers, etc.) and venues that they had been denied earlier. Starting in the second half of the 1970s, apparently, this oversight consisted of the process of *litovannia*, a procedure by which a repertoire list, along with the printed text of all song lyrics, had

---

[14]The Club of Amateur Song (Клуб Самодеятельной Песни (КСП, or KSP) was founded in Moscow in 1967. As with most Soviet scholarship, Russian bards have been written about far more extensively than Ukrainian bards such as Dmytro Kimel'feld and Leonid Dukhovyi. The first festival of Soviet Ukrainian bards occurred in 1970, but the first Ukrainian-language bards, who considered themselves "singing poets," emerged to prominence in the mid-1980s. See Rachel Platonov, "'Bad Singing': 'Avtorskaia Pesnia' and the Aesthetics of Metacommunication," *Ulbandus Review* 9 (2005), for more on the aesthetics of Soviet Russian bards.

[15]https://ua.korrespondent.net/journal/1334470-korrespondent-spivayuchi-gitari-chim-bula-avtorska-pisnya-za-chasiv-srsr-arhiv, accessed June 4, 2022.

[16]See J. Martin Daughtry, "'Sonic Samizdat': Situating Unofficial Recording in the Post-Stalinist Soviet Union," *Poetics Today* 30, no. 1 (2009).

to be submitted to a panel of experts that included representatives of Glavlit, the Union of Composers, and the Komsomol.[17]

Surprisingly little has been written into the historical record about the culture of musical *litovannia* in the post-WWII USSR, but the term came up frequently in my interviews with Ukrainian rock musicians. A generation before the era of the Kyiv Rock Club, the trailblazing Ukrainian rock band "Enei" (Еней, meaning Aeneas), who were active from 1968 to 1977, had refused to take part in official musical systems. Much of Enei's output was based on making rock arrangements of traditional Ukrainian song or the verses of Ukrainian poets; though according to Kyrylo Stetsenko, a founding member of the group, they "experimented in all of the rock trends of the time."[18] The band members—especially Taras Petrynenko, the lead singer—also wrote some original songs. Stetsenko described the inhospitable climate in which this groundbreaking Ukrainian rock band operated. "Everyone was against us," he said: the Komsomol condemned them for using corrupt "American rhythms," the Composer's Union accused them of "spitting upon the sanctity of Ukrainian song," and the KGB accused them of "bourgeois-nationalist activities," eventually forcing them to disband in 1977. But, despite this

---

[17]Aimar Ventsel, "Soviet West: Estonian *Estrada* in the Soviet Union," *Euxeinos* 8, no. 25–6 (2018) also points out the financial incentives of enforcing repertoire regulations, because the Union of Composers "collected and distributed royalty money and was therefore interested in ensuring that the songs of its members were performed as a first priority. This also explains why throughout the Soviet period the Union of Composers lobbied for the compulsory use of its members music"(100). See also Robert A. Rothstein, "The Quiet Rehabilitation of the Brick Factory: Early Soviet Popular Music and its Critics," *Slavic Review* 39, no. 3 (1980).
[18]Personal interview, January 2, 2022.

widespread hostility, Enei was invited to play frequently—at weekend dances in Bucha and Irpin, towns on the outskirts of Kyiv, or for student populations around Kyiv. It was through these youth-oriented concerts that they were able to raise enough money to purchase the necessary musical equipment normally allowed only to official groups; and as their star began to rise in the early 1970s, a shift in political winds subjected them to greater oversight from the government.

Once the grassroots support for Enei's Ukrainian rock and roll made their "amateur" activity legible to the state, they fell under greater scrutiny and had to submit to the system of *litovannia*. Stetsenko remembered a specific instance from a performance at the Kyiv Polytechnic Institute (KPI) in 1974 or 1975. After a sound check and rehearsal in the hall, the director of the hall called Stetsenko into her office and told him that Enei could not perform because their texts had not been approved, or *zalitovanni* ("не залітовані"). At that point, Stetsensko did not know what *litovannia* meant, but "implicitly understood it right away." "What's the problem?" Stetsenko asked, and he was told that Enei's songs contained "nationalist slogans." Stetsenko protested, saying there were no such slogans in their songs; that in fact the traditional texts of their songs came almost exclusively from books officially published in the USSR, and therefore vetted by Glavlit. The director claimed that one of their songs included the unsanctioned term "Mother Ukraine" (Ненька Україна). Stetsenko countered that the actual phrase he used in the original song at question was "Mother Nature" (Природа Мати), inspired by what he perceived as the environmentalist politics of the American rock band Creedence Clearwater Revival. She asked him to write these lyrics down on a piece of paper with his signature below. A bit confused, he nonetheless obliged, and she gave the approval, saying the text had now been *zalitovanno*. Stetsenko told me that Enei were savvy enough to avoid phrases that could be construed as provocative—their lead songwriter, Taras Petrynenko, waited decades before performing his song "Ukraine" (Україна), which would become a hit in the late 1980s. Nonetheless, they were harassed to remove phrases that, to him, suggested a surface-level (and rather half-hearted) ritual of compliance on the part of Soviet apparatchiks such as the director at KPI, and a deeper paranoia on the part of the state, who were trying to contain the subversive potentials of rock culture.

Litovannia was an entrenched ritual within the culture of the short-lived and Komsomol-run Kyiv Rock Club, which became the hub for "amateur" rock bands in 1986 and 1987. In order to gain access to the Kyiv Rock Club stage, a band first had to fill out an application and answer questions posed by the committee. (Tetyana Yezhova proposed that a question such as "What do you intend to say with your artistry?" could be expected.) Once admitted to the Rock Club, bands had to submit to *litovannia* before each public concert. Volodya Ivanov recalled that, "In the beginning, Komsomol members were verrrrry meticulous about the lyrics and speech of musicians, in particular during the lead up and occurrence of the 'Rock-Dialogue' festival" in April 1987.[19] Nervously scouring rock songs for subversive messages turned Komsomol apparatchiks into pests, Ivanov laughingly recalled. He described how a Russian-speaking group from Kharkiv named Utro (Morning), whose style was heavily indebted to the prog-rock of King Crimson, performed an original song whose complete lyrics consisted of one word: "Запрещено" ("Forbidden"). Ivanov reminisced, "And

---

[19]Ivanov, personal correspondence, January 2022.

the Komsomol all crowded them after the show, pressuring them to clean up the song, asking 'what does 'forbidden' mean, what does 'forbidden' mean'? And the band response was, 'Ok, the next day we will play the song with the word 'Розрішено' ('Allowed').'"

Oleg Skrypka described the "procedure of *litovannia*" as a kind of absurd farce. The procedure, according to his and others' tellings, followed approximately these rules: first, musicians would bring their song texts to a bureaucrat at the Ministry of Culture. Second, a day before the public concert, the Komsomol would set up the stage, and the band would perform in front of a committee. Skrypka recalled a committee of approximately six people sitting at a long table with a red tablecloth, dutifully following along with the printed-out lyrics. He said that it was, of course, alienating and absurd to play the full set for a panel of bureaucrats scrutinizing their punk rock songs; but for Skrypka, it was a minor nuisance. Finally, if all went according to plan, the committee would stamp the lyrics, so that if the police came to the concert the next day, the band would have these legalized texts (залітовані тексти) as proof of their right to perform.

Skrypka told me that he could not recall ever having any problems with *litovannia*. After all, they wrote "nice texts" (гарні тексти)—unobjectionable, innocuous poems about Kherson, love, and the homeland.[20] Sashko Pipa, however, recalled that in 1986, when there was a renewed Gorbachevian campaign against alcoholism, in order to legalize the text of their song "Banka" (an unreleased track from the "Tantsi" session which was released as a VV song in 2019), they had to change the word "beer" to "kvas" (the fermented non-alcoholic beverage

---

[20]Personal interview, Skrypka, June 5, 2019.

that is ubiquitous in summertime Ukraine).[21] When such demands were made, the band members acquiesced so that the concert was able to go on. As both Pipa and Skrypka affirmed separately, there was so much more going on in their music than the specific word choices in the texts, and the officials didn't understand the sarcasm; why get hung up on such a small detail?

So long as VV were classified as an "amateur" band, affiliated with the Komsomol-led Kyiv Rock Club, they had to submit to the ritual of *litovannia*. But once they left to join Rok-Artil in late 1987, they needed to obtain official status as professional musicians. As Ivanov, one of the architects of Rok-Artil told me, they were shielded "under the roof of Experiment, which gave them carte blanche as a registered musical organization, and so we did not have to continue to have the concert programs approved[22] (залітовані) and all the rest." But before they could join the Experiment, they had to be elevated from "amateur" to "professional" status, which meant participating in yet another state ritual of control: *taryfikatsia*.

Taryfikatsia: Ranks, Wages, and Rites of Passage

Taryfikatsia was a procedure enacted by Soviet bureaucrats, which, like *litovannia*, did not originate in the arena of musical labor, but was airlifted to it from other labor contexts. According to the *Academic Interpretative Dictionary of the Ukrainian*

---

[21]Personal interview, May 13, 2019.
[22]Personal interview, January 4, 2022.

Language (1970–1980), *taryfikatsia* was defined as "the determination of a tariff according to one or another classification of objects of taxation or payment. The development of technical and sound norms of production." The definition goes on to cite two specific usages of *taryfikatsia* that reveal its home context. First, an instance from *Kolhospnyk Ukraïny* (9, 1960) is given: "A correct *taryfikatsia* of work guarantees the growth of the labor activities of collective farm workers." And second, from *Komunist Ukraïny* (4, 1960, 44): "In accordance with the resolutions of the XX and XXI Congresses of the CPSU [Communist Party of the Soviet Union], the systematized improvement of the rationing and *taryfikatsia* of labor and wages results in a shortened working day."[23] In the realm of musical labor, *taryfikatsia* determined who could be registered as a "professional musician," and the level of wages they would be paid for their performances (depending on their assigned category as professionals—third, second, first, or "highest"). Categories guaranteed wages, regardless of audience turnout. Lower category musical professionals were allowed to perform in lower-status venues, such as Houses of Culture or factory clubs; higher-category musical professionals had access to more prestigious halls around the USSR and beyond. The procedure of *taryfikatsia* itself looked as follows: a committee of experts would convene to evaluate a "demonstration concert"[24] by musicians, something roughly analogous to an orchestral audition to determine whether a violinist would sit in the first, second, or nineteenth chair of the section. It was, quite literally, a method of controlling artistic production and assuring quality, in addition to standardizing

[23]This definition is archived on http://sum.in.ua/p/10/40/1, accessed January 4, 2022.
[24]Ventsel, "Soviet West: Estonian *Estrada* in the Soviet Union."

wages for state-sanctioned musical labor. If you have read this far into this book, you can probably already start to imagine how bizarre a spectacle this was in the context of VV and similar bands of the Kyiv underground.

Taryfikatsia, like *litovannia*, was introduced to music early in Soviet Ukrainian history. As far back as 1927, artists performing *estrada* (state-sanctioned popular genres) were subjected to *taryfikatsia*, a move that accompanied an intensification of state control over artistic activities.[25] Procedures of *taryfikatsia* immediately impacted the operations of musical institutions, feeding them data to help assess how musicians should be categorized and compensated. In classical music, for example, the MuzFond—the funding organization established in 1939 and controlled by Composers' Unions in each Soviet republic; who had, by the mid-1930, established a "monopol[y] on technical musical expertise" in the USSR—could refer to *taryfikatsia* results when deciding how to allocate money to musicians for material and creative support.[26] *Taryfikatsia* was a kind of rationalizing process, applied as an objective measure by which the imperatives of state cultural policies could be implemented.

Kyrylo Stetsenko encountered *taryfikatsia* personally and through his extended musical networks in Soviet Ukraine. After finishing his studies at the Kyiv Conservatory, Stetsenko became the laureate of an All-Union music competition, which won him

[25]Y.V. Mohyl'na, "Розвиток Естрадно-Вокального Мистецтва В Україні (До Історії Питання)," *Проблеми Міської Освіти* (2009), 289.
[26]See Kiril Tomoff, *Creative Union: The Professional Organization of Soviet Composers, 1939–1953* (Ithaca, N.Y.: Cornell University Press, 2006) for extensive discussion of the activities of the MuzFond, who distributed grants, stipends, and loans to musicians as well as real estate and resorts for composers' residencies. See also Boris Schwarz, *Music and Musical Life in Soviet Russia (1917–1981)* (Bloomington: Indiana University Press, 1983).

the privilege of performing as a soloist and assigned him to the first category of professionalism. Soon after, he was promoted to the highest category. Stetsenko recalled that "it was a very profitable thing, because this determined my monthly salary, which was in the highest category. And that's how it was for all working musicians." Later, when he joined the non-state sanctioned rock band Enei, *taryfikatsia* was no longer relevant, since they "operated outside of the system." His friends who performed in restaurants, however, encountered *taryfikatsia* in a slightly different way. To have the legal right to play in a restaurant, musicians had to join the local Association of Musical Ensembles. In Kyiv, the association was known as KOMA (Київське Обєднання Музичних Ансамблів); in Kharkiv, it was KhOMA (ХOMA); in L'viv, LOMA; in Odesa OOMA; and so on.[27] These associations conducted *taryfikatsia* to determine the degree and appropriate salary for restaurant musicians (even though everyone knew that musicians in restaurants made considerable extra money under the table by accepting tips for special requests). Meanwhile, the organizations known as UkrKontsert (formed in Kyiv in 1959, which directed all the philharmonics in Ukraine) and UkrEstrada (which similarly managed popular genres) also conducted *taryfikatsia* to determine ranks, salaries, and eligibility for special opportunities such as international tours.[28]

With this context in mind, imagine the absurd spectacle of a band such as VV performing a *taryfikatsia* concert. They did just this on March 23, 1988, at the hall of the publishing house "Youth" (Молодь) in Kyiv, with Kyrylo Stetsenko and Volodya

---

[27]Personal interview, Stetsenko, January 4, 2022.

[28]An entity such as UkrKontsert had analogues in other Soviet republics; in Soviet Russia, the equivalent organization was RusKontsert. These entities also existed at higher scales: SoyuzKontsert was the All-Union organization that organized concerts; GosKontsert organized international tours.

Ivanov as presenters to the assembled committee. VV performed, along with one of the other Rock Artil bands, Kollezhskyi Asessor, and an opening act. Passing the *taryfikatsia* was necessary for VV and Kollezhskyi Asessor for two reasons: first, because they sought professional status to take advantage of the new opportunities afforded by the semi-commercial collective of Rock Artil, which was housed under the umbrella of the semi-commercial collective that was sanctioned but not controlled by the Komsomol known as "Experiment" (this was described in greater detail in Chapter two). Or, as Ivanov put it, they sought to "legally leave the underground."[29] Second, because Soviet labor laws required all citizens to be registered with a legal employer, a professional affiliation would allow them to check that box. Registering as professional musicians working under the aegis of "Experiment" would thereby entitle them to be legally compensated for their musical labor.

Fortunately, this bizarre "Concert-Taryfikatsia," as it was known, has been memorialized and is available on YouTube (albeit in edited form).[30] Ivanov described the concert to me as a "hybrid" between a "juried Soviet procedure and a rock concert." Stetsenko recalled that the committee of experts represented an array of musical institutions, as well as the Komsomol. Tatyana Yezhova, who was present along with a small group of superfans selectively invited to the show, kept her recollections in a journal, reproduced here in my translation:

There are responsible people present—members of the Composers' Union of Ukraine, journalists, the Ukrainian Television. The concert is scheduled for 6:00 p.m., we arrive at

[29]Personal interview, June 8, 2022.
[30]See https://youtu.be/WiuX6Ovl1IY, last accessed June 15, 2022.

> 4:30 p.m. On the stage, Kollezhskyi Asessor was setting up; behind the console was Dima Maziuk, the current sound guy for Kollezhskyi Asessor. We go backstage and encounter [Volodya] Ivanov, who immediately gives us our orders ... I carry our coats to VV's room and exchange a few words with Yura [Zdorenko]. Skrypka tries on a cap, in which he would later perform a song, and then the cap is put on Ivanov. After some time, people start to gather. I am introduced to Mark Anapolsky, a representative of the L'viv Rock Club. We share all kinds of information. The hall is full ... the concert begins.[31]

After briefly reviewing the first two acts (a band called Slovoposlie whom she finds quite derivative, and Kollezhskyi Asessor, whom she admires), VV takes the stage. Yezhova dwells on their performance in detail:

> VV. The guys are growing; and if this isn't worthy of praise, then it's better not to watch or listen to them at all. Half of the program was new. A few of the songs are influenced by Soviet *estrada* of the early 1970s. Skrypka picked up the guitar. Of the older songs—"Tantsi," "Pisen'ka," "Zadnye Oko," and "Yaroslavna's Lament." We probably won't hear the song "On Duty" anymore; Yura told me about this when we sat at Café "Sevastopol," since this song had aged out of fashion ... Of the new songs—"Zarathustra"—which probably has a different name ... in Ukrainian.[32] Skrypka with maracas in his hands making Indian dance moves. Shura [Sashko Pipa] and especially Yura have stopped being restrained on stage. Yura jumped, even made a "goat" once, probably remembering his

---

[31] Read it in the original Russian at: http://vopli.blogspot.com/2008/11/1988_16.html. This is my translation from the Russian.
[32] This references the song known as "Mahatma."

past as a metalhead.[33] On one of the songs they let on Kotenko-Baton, but he was in a deranged state.[34] VV performed twenty-one songs. It was a wonderful performance … [35] VV was videotaped; Asessor too, it seems.

The video of the performance begins formally, with the four band members walking onto stage. Skrypka wears an oversized black suit and a light red shirt underneath; later in the performance, he removes his jacket to reveal suspenders holding up his roomy suit-pants. Pipa and Zdorenko, oddly, crowd stage left for the entirety of the show (stage right is vacant), emphasizing their discrepancy in height. Pipa, with a dapper rockabilly pompadour, wears a threadbare red tank top; Zdorenko is in something like a flannel shirt, with his signature "proletarian beret" atop his head. Sakhno, the drummer, is hidden behind Skrypka until the end of the performance, but one can occasionally see him collecting the sticks that have fallen to the floor in the course of play. The performance alternates—often without warning—between deadpan calm and utter mania, with the musicians jolting out of near immobility to exaggerated and often goofy dance moves, sometimes posing heroically, then shifting in a flash into full body movement.

The first song of their set is their hit, "Tantsi." Skrypka introduces the song with stylized formality, mimicking the

---

[33]The "goat" most likely refers to the "devil-horns" hand sign popularized by the heavy metal singer Ronnie James Dio.

[34]Most likely a reference to the Mohawked punk who danced on stage for much of the song "Olia."

[35]Yezhova also noted that this was only "the second performance of VV with lights in an auditorium. The first time was at the Kyiv Institute of Civil Aviation Engineers (КНИГА, one of the halls the held rock concerts in the late 1980s and early 1990s) … "

Figure 4.2 *A scene from VV's Concert–Taryfikatsia, 1988. Screenshot from YouTube.*

happy talk of Soviet authoritative speech and flowing directly into the opening of the song: "Good evening, dear friends. I inform you that you are watching VV, and the last thing I will say is '*The day ends / It surrenders its hopes to the night* ... '" The stage is framed by a banner hung high that reads "Rock Artil," and as "Tantsi" kicks into its groove, the iconic "Tantsi" banner is carried onto stage by a pair of punks. (According to Ivanov, this concert may have marked the first appearance of the banner, which he manufactured in his artist's studio.) In the second song on the video, the high-energy "Olia," a punk with a glorious spiked mohawk—probably the same Kotenko-Baton referenced in Yezhova's journal—leaps on to the stage and dances next to Skrypka, who occasionally syncs to his moves. The camera, meanwhile, meanders away from the spirited youth crowding the front of the hall to reveal rows of quietly seated spectators, likely the committee that would decide whether VV would pass the *taryfikatsia* and be recognized as professionals.

The concert proceeds with high-octane energy. The penultimate song is the premiere of "Mahatma," followed by a performance of "Yaroslavna's Lament," the song that controversially won "Best Song of the Year" at the Kyiv Rock Club's Rock Parade Festival in 1987 (as described in Chapter two). When the set ends, Skrypka bows theatrically, and Sakhno emerges from behind the drum kit to line up next to his bandmates. Ivanov comes on to stage, joined later by Stetsenko. As the small crowd cheers wildly, Ivanov announces the names of the four musicians, and then triumphantly proclaims, "We're happy to acquaint you with our Soviet punk rock!"

But this moment of elation was quickly deflated when the committee moved into its deliberation. After a heated two-hour debate, the committee voted against all the bands. Yezhova told me in 2021 that she still remembers clearly how an older man, a representative of the Ministry of Culture—"a real, official Soviet guy"—stood up and said, "Boys, how are you not ashamed to mock the Ukrainian language!" Yezhova described more in her journal entry:

> After the concert, a discussion took place. It lasted almost two hours. I risked staying in the room for fifteen minutes, and then left. The groups did not pass the *taryfikatsia*. It seems that none of these comrades need a "Rock Artil." Ivanov represented VV, Ivankevych—Rabbota XO, Hoidenko—Asessor … [36] A dozen people courageously

---

[36]Viktor Ivankevych was the official representative of the Rock Artil collective at the time. Hoidenko was the leader of Kollezhskyi Asessor.

waited for the end of the conversation, after which four people, including myself, went over to Sasha Lytovka's place to worry.[37] We talked until 2:00 a.m., and at half past three we caught a taxi. Ivanov initiated me into the punks and said that I was getting "more and more cool." These are, of course, jokes.

As Yezhova's story shows, although the rite of official passage may have been unsuccessful, the night nonetheless intensified the bonds between this community of *neformaly*, who stood in clearer opposition than before to the old guard of Soviet institutions.

And tellingly, after some insignificant amount of time passed, VV and the other bands of Rock Artil somehow *did* get the papers, stamps, and approvals they needed to continue their work with Rock Artil legally. As with Stetsenko's story about the half-hearted litovannia of Enei's texts, there were workarounds to rites of *taryfikatsia* in the era of *perestroika*.

Politrok, or Trolling the Komsomol

According to Volodya Ivanov, VV's first manager, the band "trolled the Komsomol" expertly with their parodic style.[38] Take the song "Politrok," introduced on the *Tantsi* recordings by Oleg Skrypka—who proclaims, with boozy confidence, "Political Rock and Roll"! while another band member laughs in the background. He proclaims it twice more before the song kicks

---

[37]Yezhova explains that Aleksandr Lytovka was the "chairman of the friendly Rock Artil association known as the "Musical Living Room," comprised of non-musicians who supported Rock Artil.
[38]Personal interview, January 4, 2022.

in. To my ears, the song's provocative title is made comical by Skrypka's repetition of "Rock"!—punctuated with full band hits—at the end of each enigmatic verse. The following is our attempt to translate the spare text of the song as it was performed on the *Tantsi* album:

We play
The music of the day,
We play about that which bothers everyone,
Politrok,
Politrok.
We—you
Rock! Rock!

You see it everywhere,
You see it in us.
Everyone will make their own conclusions.
Politrok,
Politrok.
Everywhere—around us
Rock! Rock!

[Spoken] Everyone will make their own conclusions!

We do not have time and
There are no alternatives.
What is insufficient?
Who did what?
Here you go
Rock! Rock!

In the store what?
In the store—shish![39]
We'll sing all together
Politrok,
Politrok.
What? Shish!
Rock! Rock! Rock!

The notion suggested in the first verse—that *politrok*, or political rock, is what "bothers everyone"—may refer to the panic over rock and roll discussed earlier in the chapter, or it may not.[40] The second verse uses the plural "you" case in Ukrainian, which is the same grammatical form used to address people of high status, though it could also be addressing multiple "yous" of ordinary status. That verse also allows for the possibility of multiple interpretations of politrok, that which is "seen everywhere," as if to provoke an already paranoid Komsomol. Skrypka repeats that line over the instrumental break. The third and fourth verses seem to gesture towards the scarcity of the Soviet economy during the final years of its existence, culminating in clipped answers to the cryptic questions posed. One interpretation of this song was suggested to me in the following way: "Oh so you want to politicize our music? It's already political, just not how you

[39]The ambiguous slang term they use here is "шиш." One of the possible meanings of the term relates to a gesture in which the hand makes a fist, with the thumb protruding between the second and third fingers, roughly meaning something like "nuts to you." It can also simply be the gesture known as "'flipping the bird".

[40]Sashko Pipa says that "Politrok" was written in response to the late awakening of Russian rock groups who were just starting to become more openly critical of Soviet rule. For Ukrainian groups, this was like noticing—in Pipa's words—"that water is wet." (Personal correspondence, November 29, 2022).

think." To a nervous Komsomol apparatchik, or a serious composer in the Composer's Union, or a bureaucrat in the Ministry of Culture, or to anyone tasked with censoring rock music, "Politrok" is expert trolling—just vague enough to plausibly reject claims that it is mocking Soviet authority.

Ivanov, who represented VV as their manager, also told me joyfully that he "trolled them too"! He shared an anecdote about how the band's name, VV, scared the Komsomol initially. "Vopli Vidopliassova" (which, again, means "the wailings of Vidopliassov," based on a character from Dostoevsky's *The Village of Stepanchikovo*) became quickly abbreviated among Kyivan rockers to "Ve-Ve." At that time, the First Secretary of the Communist Party of Ukraine was Volodymyr Vasylyovych Shcherbytsky, who was also apparently referred to in Communist Party jargon as "Ve-Ve." Ivanov talked about how, as the "first point of contact with the Komsomol" in his capacity as manager, he had to repeatedly reassure them that the name was not in fact a play on the Communist leader's name, but really a somewhat ludicrous homage to a minor Dostoevskian character. But he delighted in keeping them confused—signaling that actually there was a hidden meaning, and then assuring them there was not. Ivanov goaded them to perform their uncertainty over and over, just because he could.

Ivanov's low-stakes cat-and-mouse game with Komsomol leaders captures something at once mundane and profound about the overarching story here—about how Komsomol apparatchiks and punk rockers fostered tenuous alliances. These alliances were not built on trust and respect, but rather on some degree of suspicion and opportunism—both sides shared an ambition to get something out of the system as it existed. In sustaining these alliances, the Komsomol admitted new forms of expression into late Soviet life, pushing the definition of what could still count as state-sanctioned music. In a period of tumult and transformation, in which high-level officials deliberated in official meetings over how to solve the "problem of rock and roll" in late Soviet Ukraine, such alliances became life rafts, harbors of anarchic creativity floating in the gasping, churning waters of late Soviet society.

5 Conclusion: *Tantsi* Forever

Oksana Susyak was the first self-proclaimed Ukrainian *neformalka* I ever met. I met her in 2008, far from the milieu of late Soviet Kyiv in time and space, at her rural home ringed by the Carpathian Mountains in the west of Ukraine. I admired how she lived her nonconformist lifestyle in an unlikely place; she appreciated my interest in the culture of her hometown. We bonded quickly, and I came to rent a small cottage at her family homestead on and off for the next two years while I pursued the research for my first book, *Wild Music: Sound and Sovereignty in Ukraine*, an ethnography of Ukrainian musical practices in various borderland regions of Ukraine.

A spunky and gritty woman with a punk-inflected personal style, Oksana had been raised by a single mother, immersed in the social life of her traditional Hutsul community in the small mountain town of Verkhovyna. As a teenager, Oksana applied for college in Kyiv. She fell in love with the big city and spent the next two decades as part of the Kyivan *tusovka*, palling around with hip young artists, rockers, and filmmakers. In the volatile post-Soviet 1990s, Oksana seized on new financial possibilities and took a job for a powerful oligarch, a position that bankrolled her cosmopolitan lifestyle and afforded her opportunities to travel internationally—to Tunisia, Germany, Bulgaria. But those years were also accompanied by an awakening: as the Soviet archives opened, Oksana devoured new publications that uncovered a history of the repression of the Ukrainian language, of the mass execution of Ukrainian cultural leaders during the Soviet period, and of the quashing of various pro-Ukrainian political movements. By 1997, she had come to the decision to switch from speaking Russian—the language of business as well as of her social circle—to Ukrainian. Her friends teased her about her linguistic conversion. Oksana remembers how one close friend said, "What, you can't speak in a normal language? Should I start speaking in Chinese now?" But they tolerated Oksana's linguistic conversion as a temporary eccentricity. The phase, though, did not pass; instead, her pro-Ukrainian sentiments deepened. Eventually—telling herself she needed to oversee the installation of modern plumbing at her mother's home—she moved back to Verkhovyna permanently.

There, Oksana refashioned herself as a local activist, small business owner, and artist. But she maintained a strong connection to Kyiv, traveling back annually for many years to attend its "Molodist" film festival, regularly hosting her Kyivan friends at her artsy Carpathian home and advancing various projects of "Ukrainianizing" her old friends with humor and love.

Oksana's story may appear a neat, even extreme, case of awakening to one's Ukrainian identity, but her story is by no means unique. I was drawn to write about this particular late Soviet VV album—with its linguistically hybrid, politically ambiguous, endlessly irreverent shtick—in part because it epitomizes the messy and contradictory conditions by which many Ukrainians have come into awareness of themselves *as* Ukrainian over time: by choice, by circumstance, or even by accident. (I recognize myself, with my own hybrid Ukrainian-American identification, as a person who has grown over time into greater identification with the Ukrainian side of the hyphen.) As the brutal Russian war of aggression against Ukraine rages on, allowing Ukrainians some of this complexity strikes me as critical if we wish to see Ukraine survive. This means recognizing that Ukrainians exist in a web of meanings as dense as the rest of us. It means that those Ukrainians committed to being Ukrainian may do so for a mix of reasons unknown to us, for reasons far less clear-cut than the caricatures that circulate in warring media environments. The Kremlin offers us the following options for understanding who Ukrainians are: one, Ukrainians have always been screeching nationalists, now turned murderous neo-Nazis; two, Ukrainians are actually Russians temporarily suffering from false consciousness. Much Western media offers us similarly limited, if diametrically opposed, alternatives: one, Ukrainians are the selfless defenders of liberal democratic values; two, they are the selfless defenders of libertarian ideals of "freedom;" in both cases, they are pure vessels martyring themselves so that "we" (in the West) may rediscover our own higher ideals. None of these caricatures capture anything close to the full and "complex personhood"[1] of the Ukrainians I know, including those whose experiences were represented throughout this book.

Accidental Politics and Underground Continuities

In the 1980s, VV were hardly Ukrainian nationalists, but they did spark something like a flicker of Ukrainian awareness, an accidental politics, among many punks and metalheads of

---

[1] For a compelling definition of "complex personhood," see Avery Gordon, *Ghostly Matters: Haunting and the Sociological Imagination* (Minneapolis: University of Minnesota Press, 2008: 4–5).

their scene—even as they were decried by more pearl-clutching segments of Ukrainian society. Their former manager, Volodya Ivanov, summarized it this way: "there were, of course, insults from the conservative '*sharovarna*[2] public that VV was 'smearing the Ukrainian language', or that 'they depict Ukrainians as peasants' and that sort of thing (surprisingly, this happens even now!), but for creative youth, VV often became a kind of 'flag' and a model." Eugene Hütz, then a teenage superfan, described how VV "helped the wheels turn" for many young people in that scene. When I asked whether he perceived VV, at the time, as making fun of Ukrainians, he answered with this:

> Well, it's like this. I could see if you were coming from the guardian echelon of Ukrainian culture it could spook you out because of its eccentricity and surrealistic take on things. But you gotta understand that, at the same time, these were also the guys who went to Moscow and blew everyone's minds off because they were singing in Ukrainian. It was a statement on behalf of Ukrainian culture. No one there perceived it as making fun of anything, just like *wow, this shit is for real*. So, I think it played a positive role. Especially in Kyiv, you know, where at the time, and it's sad to admit, but there were a lot of people who were kind of drifting away from even understanding that Kyiv was a Ukrainian city. The Soviets did a lot of shit to fuck it up, you know! So having anything in Ukrainian, even if it had kitschy elements about it, was still positive. And you still had kids with тризуби [tridents, the national insignia of Ukraine] inside of their leather jackets

---

[2]A term indicating Ukrainians committed to a pristine and quasi-folkloric vision of Ukrainian culture.

gathering around and discussing the topic like "yo, this is my shit."[3]

I share these perspectives not to prove that some essential Ukrainian-ness was always latent, bubbling beneath the surface and waiting to be triumphantly liberated after the fall of the USSR. That story would hew dangerously close to the Whiggish "triumph of the resisting subject" narratives that have defined so much scholarship on the Soviet past, often by implicitly or explicitly doubling down on the cult of liberal individuality.[4] Such resistance narratives risk obscuring the collective dynamics at stake in forging a story of self; or how a slow coming into collective self-recognition could bring us to the point (as I write this) that a substantial contingent of the same punk kids who were hanging together at the Rock Artil *tusovka* in the late 1980s are today volunteering in the territorial defense, serving in the Ukrainian Armed Forces, or tirelessly touring to raise funds and awareness for humanitarian, medical, defensive, and other causes—despite the repeated failures of the post-Soviet Ukrainian state to secure stability and dignity for its citizens.

Whatever we make of VV's intention at the time, the effect of *Tantsi*—a semi-official cassette release that spread "Veve-mania" throughout Ukraine in the last years of the USSR[5] —was to seed an accidental politics in the late 1980s that resonated after the fall, into the 1990s, and continues to proliferate even today. VV's early punk message became one small element in

---

[3]Personal interview, February 3, 2022.
[4]Krylova, "The Tenacious Liberal Subject in Soviet Studies."
[5]Yevtushenko concretely links the spread of what he terms "Veve-mania" to VV's earliest cassette releases (2011, 142).

a larger story of Ukrainians reclaiming their language, their culture, and their historical inheritances, while simultaneously revising the outsider narratives that had always been imposed through the gaze of various imperial formations.

VV's own post-Soviet track record of mining their late Soviet materials spurred multiple waves of reflection about what it had all meant. VV's 2006 album *There Were Days*—which presented the first high-quality studio recordings of many of the songs that first circulated in recorded form on the *Fonohraf* cassette dub of *Tantsi* in 1989—put Oleksandr Yevtushenko, the late chronicler of the Kyiv rock scene, in a nostalgic mood. He described how back "in those uncertain and foggy times, the boys couldn't get access to a decent studio for recording their hot material," and so the 2006 record was an attempt to recapture the "old VV that was by now shrouded in myth and legend."Yevtushenko considered the 2006 project conceptual, an "emotional journey to restore the classic VV sound" and to "send us back into recent history so that we can once again immerse ourselves in those unforgettable days in Kyiv."[6] This project of time-traveling to the sweaty Kyiv *tusovka* was, for Yevtushenko, intimately connected with the emergence of a Ukrainian popular music scene that young urbanites like him could claim proudly as their own.

The spirit of that late Soviet Ukrainian music scene also crossed the Atlantic, embodied in the immigration stories of people such as Eugene Hütz. Hütz, who came of age in the Kyiv punk scene and emigrated to Vermont with his family in December of 1989, described how his experiences in late Soviet Ukraine helped him find a familiar new scene in his

[6]Yevtushenko 2011, 69–70.

Figure 5.1 *"After Tantsi," published in* Fonohraf. *From the personal archives of O. Rudiachenko. Used with permission.*

American home. The network of zines and the bible of DIY touring, *Book Your Own Fucking Life* (BYOFL), all felt like familiar resources, familiar ad hoc infrastructures. These continuities came as a pleasant surprise:

> The amazing thing is that what we thought was hard, you
> know—you have no support to organize any show, you

basically had to drag your drums through the subway on your back—when I came here to the States I basically went straight to the same environment. Like, I was completely into punk rock, but when I got here the hard-core scene just swept me off my feet because they were so all-inclusive. So I went straight to the same thing, you know, lugging fucking drums on my back and playing God knows where in like basements and kitchens, throughout the whole 1990s. The vibe here was very similar to the *Huchnomovets* vibe. Like Ian MacKaye from Fugazi just might as well be a guy from Rock Artil, you know? It's just very DIY, don't wait for anybody, nobody's going to do it for you, don't make it to be a real business, because fuck real business, because it's not about this, because it's mostly going to be art and your family.

Having found his new scene, Hütz began to integrate elements from his Kyivan upbringing into his new bands, drawing inspiration from VV's histrionic performances and unapologetically hybrid argot.

"Tantsi" the song has also been reinvented—imitated, parodied, covered—numerous times. A 2019 cover version of the iconic "Tantsi" music video testifies to its enduring relevance. In it, Ivan Dorn, a popular Ukrainian singer, performed as Skrypka, with other musicians cast as Zdorenko, Pipa, and Sakhno. Dorn and the others studiously mimed the manic movements of the original VV lineup, though their very studiousness kept them from inhabiting the zany energy of the original. It was an eerie exercise to remake this trailblazing music video in 2019, a neat thirty years after its rise to prominence, but an exercise that reveals the lasting impact of an improvised music video that sparked a public controversy, and something like an earthquake.[7] In 2007, the folk-punk band Yurcash released a song titled "Tantsi 2 3.3 VV," in joking homage to the VV original. The lyrics reminisce about those golden years ("Oh, how beautifully they played the dances of Vopli Vidopliassova / I remember clubs playing rock over the *huchnomovets'* (loudspeakers)") but wryly note that "Oleg Skrypka was dragged into mass culture" after the fact. The song ends with the repetition of a phrase reminiscent of Soviet sloganeering: "Let him dance, let him sing, the rock legend of Vopli / Just as long as there's no war."[8] In the combination parody and homage, an enduring love for "Tantsi" is married to a critique of post-Soviet capitalism and the persistent threat of war.

But the afterlife of *Tantsi*, it turns out, was not merely conceptual.

Long Live *Tantsi*, or, Хай Живе *Танці*

Sashko Pipa showed me around Akademmistechko. From outside the gates of the Institute of Metallurgy, he pointed out the window closest to where VV set up their recording rig for the *Tantsi* sessions. Pipa explained the contours of the neighborhood where they had lived, and then we settled into the sunny terrace

---

[7]The original video and the 2019 remake are shown side-by-side in the following YouTube video: https://www.youtube.com/watch?v=sc6URhv0L4 A&t=7s (accessed January 8, 2022).

[8]I thank Pavlo Hrytsak for helping me decode some of these lyrics. The phrase "Хай танцює, хай співає рок-легенда Воплів / Аби не було війни" is dense with syntax suggestive of Soviet authoritative speak. Needless to say, the line "Just as long as there's no war"—a formulaic slogan from Soviet times, written into this song at a time of relative peace—rings differently in 2022.

Figure 5.2 *Sashko Pipa with the VV master tape, Akademmistechko, Kyiv, 2019. Photo by M. Sonevytsky.*

of a sushi restaurant. It was May 2019, and Pipa had brought a surprise, excavated from his closet, to our interview: the original master tape of the *Tantsi* session that led to the *Fonohraf* cassette release in March 1989. Pipa told me that the fact that they had recorded on a West German reel—produced by the company known by the acronym BASF—and not on Soviet tape was the reason it had not turned to dust in the intervening decades.

I immediately asked him whether the reel had ever been properly digitized. Pipa responded that it had not. That evening, I brainstormed with my husband, the musician and writer Franz Nicolay, about potential reissue labels that could do right by *Tantsi*. Org Music, an innovative California-based label led by the punk enthusiast Andrew Rossiter, expressed interest in the project, and I brought it to the stakeholders in the band to see if they would get on board. They did.

After considerable delay because of the global pandemic, I travelled back to Kyiv in October 2021 on a mission to retrieve the master tape from Sashko Pipa and transport it safely back to the US. Once it had passed through the hands of the audio wizards at Infrasonic Mastering, I had the first opportunity to listen to the raw audio of the digitized tape in late October 2021. We listened in my husband's home studio, and he immediately remarked: "It really feels like you're in the room." I honestly did feel transported, imagining these young men with nothing to lose, their full-throttle energy overwhelming the dinky recording space that they had carved out inside the Institute of Metallurgy in Akademmistechko. It was sheer thrill to hear these songs fresh, recorded thirty years earlier in a city I love, to experience the deep pleasures encoded in tape. The remastered *Tantsi* session is scheduled to receive its first "official" release in spring 2023, in tandem with the publication of this book.

Tantsi lives on. It endures in the ways it inspired people in the Kyiv *tusovka* who heard something that they could claim as their own and prompted new and often idiosyncratic ways of identifying as Ukrainian, with existential stakes for the country. *Tantsi* endures in the ways it allowed those in the Ukrainian diasporas—those of us whose families scattered across the world to escape violence and repression in earlier generations—to recognize ourselves not only in our immigrant enclaves, but in modern Ukraine as well. *Tantsi* endures in the fans it won, not just within Ukraine or the USSR, but in Western Europe, breaking new ground for Ukrainian musicians. And *Tantsi* endures as an irrepressibly human response to bleak times, with its insistence on irreverent fun, its dare to cut loose. Viva *Tantsi*.

Bibliography

Bahry, Romana. "Rock Culture and Rock Music in Ukraine." In *Rocking the State: Rock Music and Politics in Eastern Europe and Russia*, edited by Sabrina P. Ramet. Boulder: Westview Press, 1994.

Bahry, Romana. "The Satirical Current in Popular Youth Culture: Rock Music and Film in Ukraine in the 1990s." Paper presented at Ukraine in the 1990s: Proceedings of the First Conference of the Ukrainian Studies Association of Monash University, Monash University, 24–6 January 1992.

Bilaniuk, Laada. *Contested Tongues: Language Politics and Cultural Correction in Ukraine.* Ithaca, NY: Cornell University Press, 2005.

Boyer, Dominic and Alexei Yurchak. "American Stiob: Or, What Late-Socialist Aesthetics of Parody Reveal about Contemporary Political Culture in the West." *Cultural Anthropology* 25, no. 2 (2010): 179–221.

Boym, Svetlana. *The Future of Nostalgia.* New York: Basic Books, 2001.

Cushman, Thomas. *Notes from Underground: Rock Music Counterculture in Russia.* Albany: State University of New York Press, 1995.

Daughtry, J. Martin. "Russia's New Anthem and the Negotiation of National Identity." *Ethnomusicology* 47, no. 1 (2003): 42–67.

Daughtry, J. Martin.. "'Sonic Samizdat': Situating Unofficial Recording in the Post-Stalinist Soviet Union." *Poetics Today* 30, no. 1 (Spring 2009): 27–65.

Fürst, Juliane. "Liberating Madness–Punishing Insanity: Soviet Hippies and the Politics of Craziness." *Journal of Contemporary History* 53, no. 4 (2018): 832–60.

Gordon, Avery. *Ghostly Matters: Haunting and the Sociological Imagination*. Minneapolis: University of Minnesota Press, 2008.

Helbig, Adriana. "Ukraine." In *The International Recording Industries*, edited by Lee Marshall, 192–206. London: Routledge, 2013.

Herzfeld, Michael. *Cultural Intimacy*: Social Poetics in the Nation-State. London: Routledge, 2004.

Kielman, Adam. "Sonic Infrastructures, Musical Circulation and Listening Practices in a Changing People's Republic of China." *Sound Studies* 4, no. 1 (2018): 19–34.

Krylova, Anna. "The Tenacious Liberal Subject in Soviet Studies." *Kritika: Explorations in Russian and Eurasian History* 1, no. 1 (2000): 119–46.

Kushnir, Alexander. *100 Magnitoalbomov Sovetkogo Roka. 1977–1991: 15 Let Podpol'noi Zvukozapysy*. Moscow: Agraf, 1999.

Memmi, Albert. *The Colonizer and the Colonized*. London: Earthscan Publications Ltd, 2003 [1957].

Mohyl'na, Y.V. "Розвиток Естрадно-Вокального Мистецтва В Україні (До Історії Питання)." *Проблеми Міської Оствіти* (2009).

Mukharskyi, Antin. *Жлобологія*. Київ: Наш Формат, 2013.

Platonov, Rachel. "'Bad Singing': 'Avtorskaia Pesnia' and the Aesthetics of Metacommunication." *Ulbandus Review* 9 (2005): 87–113.

Platt, Kevin, and Benjamin Nathans. "Socialist in Form, Indeterminate in Content: The Ins and Outs of Late Soviet Culture." *Ab Imperio* 2011 (2011): 301–24.

Portnov, Andrii. "Memory Wars in Post-Soviet Ukraine (1991–2010)." In *Memory and Theory in Eastern Europe*, edited by Uilleam Blacker, Alexander Etkind, and Julie Fedor, 233–54. New York: Palgrave Macmillan, 2013.

Rivkin-Fish, Michele. "Tracing Landscapes of the Past in Class Subjectivity: Practices of Memory and Distinction in Marketizing Russia." *American Ethnologist* 36, no. 1 (2009): 79–95.

Rothstein, Robert A. "The Quiet Rehabilitation of the Brick Factory: Early Soviet Popular Music and its Critics." *Slavic Review* 39, no. 3 (1980): 373–88.

Sakwa, Richard. *Gorbachev and His Reforms (1985–1990)*. 2nd ed. New York: Prentice Hall, 1991.

Schwarz, Boris. *Music and Musical Life in Soviet Russia (1917–1981)*. Bloomington: Indiana University Press, 1983.

Scott, James C. *Weapons of the Weak: Everyday Forms of Peasant Resistance*. New Haven: Yale University Press, 1985.

Sharafutdinova, Gulnaz. "Was There a 'Simple Soviet' Person? Debating the Politics and Sociology of 'Homo Sovieticus.'" *Slavic Review* 78, no. 1 (2019): 173–95.

Shevchuk, Yuri I. *Ukrainian-English Collocation Dictionary*. New York: Hippocrene Books, 2021.

Stavyts'ka, Lesia. *Ukrainskiy Zharhon*. Kyiv: Krytyka, 2005.

Tomoff, Kiril. *Creative Union: The Professional Organization of Soviet Composers, 1939–1953*. Ithaca, N.Y.: Cornell University Press, 2006.

Troitsky, Artemy. *Tusovka : Who's Who in the New Soviet Rock Culture*. London and New York: Omnibus Press 1990.

Ventsel, Aimar. "Soviet West: Estonian *Estrada* in the Soviet Union." *Euxeinos* 8, no. 25–6 (2018): 94–106.

Wanner, Catherine Cowhey. *Burden of Dreams: History and Identity in Post-Soviet Ukraine*. Post-Communist Cultural Studies. University Park, PA: Pennsylvania State Univ. Press, 1998.

Yevtushenko, Oleksandr M. *Ukraïna IN ROCK*. De Profundis. Kyiv: Hrani-T, 2011.

Yurchak, Alexei. *Everything Was Forever, Until It Was No More: The Last Soviet Generation*. Princeton, NJ: Princeton University Press, 2005.

Yurchak, Alexei. "Gagarin and the Rave Kids: Transforming Power, Identity, and Aesthetics in the Post-Soviet Night Life." In *Consuming Russia: Popular Culture, Sex, and Society since Gorbachev*, edited by A. Baker, 76–109. Durham: Duke University Press, 1999.

Yurchak, Alexei. "A Parasite from Outer Space: How Sergei Kurekhin Proved That Lenin Was a Mushroom." *Slavic Review* 70, no. 2 (2011): 307–33.

Zemtsovsky, Izaly. "Musicological Memoirs on Marxism." Translated by Katherine Durnin. In *Music & Marx: Ideas, Practice, Politics*, edited by Regula Burckhardt Qureshi, 167–89. New York and London: Routledge, 2002.

Zhuk, Sergei I. "'The Disco Mafia' and 'Komsomol Capitalism' in Soviet Ukraine During Late Socialism." In *Material Culture in Russia and the USSR*, 173–95: Routledge, 2020.

Zhuk, Sergei I. "Fascist Music from the West: Anti-Rock Campaigns, Problems of National Identity, and Human Rights in the 'Closed City' of Soviet Ukraine, 1975–84." Chap. 11 In *Popular Music and Human Rights: Volume II: World Music* edited by Ian Peddie, 147–59. London: Routledge, 2011.

Zubok, Vladislav M. *Collapse: The Fall of the Soviet Union*. New Haven: Yale University Press, 2021.

INDEX

Enei (rock band) 34 n.5,
117–19, 124, 130
estrada (Soviet state-sanctioned
pop music) 16, 22, 77, 89,
123, 126
see also UkrEstrada
"ethno-punk" 6
see also rock styles,
subgenres
"evil empire" 8
exorcism 26, 83
"Experiment" (cooperative) xxii,
59–60, 108, 121, 125
see also Rock Artil

fascism, fascist
Banderites and 71 n.14
"fascist punks" 103–4
fashion 4 n.3, 78, 79, 127
festival
Chervona Ruta xxiv, 42,
108
Debut '86 xx, 43
"Molodist" Film Festival xxi,
57, 136
Rock Dialogue xxi, 57, 119
Rock Parade 55, 60, 129
folklore 21, 77, 78, 92–3,
109–10
Fonohraf
circular economy 38–48
as cooperative 12, 20, 35–6,
43–4
Digest (1989) xxv, 41, 54
in *Moloda Gvardia*
newspaper 38–42
France 7, 57–8, 58 n.36

see also "Rock Around the
Kremlin" (French TV
documentary)
Fürste, Juliane 83

glasnost (openness) xx, 9,
109 n.8, 115
Glavlit (Main Directorate for the
Protection of State
Secrets in the Press and
other Mass Media) 115,
117, 118
Gnativ, Oleg (aka Mokh) 21, 50
Gogol Bordello 9, 11, 50
Gorbachev, Mikhail xix, 38
Gorbachev's reforms 9, 35, 37,
43, 55, 103
see also perebudova, glasnost
guitar
bass guitar 2, 10–11, 18, 82;
see also Pipa, Sashko
"dust-covered guitar sound"
96
hero 95
lead guitar 2, 22, 65, 98; see
also Zdorenko, Yuri
as "snow shovel" 11
solo 4
Gutgarts, Gennady 88–9, 90–1

"heroic style" 96
homo sovieticus 23, 77, 85–6
Huchnomovets
lyric in "Pisen'ka" 91, 93
lyric in "Tantsi 2 3.3 VV" 143
samizdat zine xxii, 36, 48–53,
59, 63, 142